ARKANSAS \
GUIDE

MW00998932

BY TIM ERNST

Please note that most waterfalls in Arkansas are "wet-weather" falls.
They generally do not flow all year long,
and are almost always dry in the summer and fall months.

It is important that you read the entire introduction before attempting
to locate any of the waterfalls described in this guidebook.

All of the photographs in this book are available as color prints
in a variety of sizes, with or without the person in the photo.
For details on how to order go to **www.Cloudland.net.**

CLOUDLAND.NET PUBLISHING
CAVE MOUNTAIN, ARKANSAS

*The photo on the front cover is of Triple Falls (aka Twin Falls) at Camp Orr in the
Buffalo River drainage. The hiker is Pam Ernst (who drew all of the maps in this
guidebook). See page 60 for the map and directions to this fall.*

1

Library of Congress Control Number: 2002094418
ISBN 1–882906–48–9

Book designed by Tim Ernst
Other Production Team Members:
Pam Ernst, Norma Senyard, Sara Eisenbacher, Judy Ferguson, Glenn Wheeler

Wilderness publications by Tim Ernst

Arkansas Hiking Trails guidebook
Buffalo River Hiking Trails guidebook
Ozark Highlands Trail guidebook
Ouachita Trail guidebook
Arkansas Dayhikes For Kids guidebook
Arkansas Waterfalls guidebook

Arkansas Wilderness picture book
Buffalo River Wilderness picture book
Arkansas Spring picture book
Arkansas Portfolio picture book
Wilderness Reflections picture book

The Search For Haley

Limited-edition posters, prints and calendars
(all of the photos in this guidebook
are available as color prints in a variety of sizes)

Items may be ordered direct from:
Tim Ernst
HC 33, Box 50–A
Pettigrew, Arkansas   72752 (Cave Mountain)
Toll-free order line: 800–838–HIKE
Web Page: **www.Cloudland.net**

See page 222 for book prices.

WARNING:
Visiting waterfalls may be hazardous to your health!

By their very nature and location, waterfalls can be dangerous to be around. There are many hazards that can cause accidents, resulting in serious injury or death. It is not the intent of this guidebook—nor any of the directions or recommendations presented here—that when followed will assure safe passage to or from any waterfall. Many of the descriptions suggest backcountry routes over rugged and dangerous terrain, where there are no trails—significant experience with travel under these conditions is suggested.

It is understood that if you pick up and read this guidebook and use the information contained within to venture out into the wilderness to visit these waterfalls, that you do so at your own risk, with full knowledge of your own limitations, and that no matter what you do, there is a possibility of serious injury or death, and that you accept and are responsible for your own actions and safety. The author, publisher, and any re-seller cannot and do not accept any liability resulting from the material in this book. If you do not agree with any of the above, please return this book to the shelf and stay home!

If you want to take your **KIDS** with you to visit these waterfalls, please choose which ones you visit wisely—the high bluffs around the falls require that you *pay close attention to your children at all times* and *hold onto them*. It is up to the parents to decide which waterfalls are suitable—see the note on page 9. Some waterfalls that may be more kid-friendly than others are noted in the Table of Contents, but it is recommended that parents visit each waterfall first to decide for themselves. We want our youth to experience the great natural beauty that is around us, but we also want to keep them alive—they are the future of the world!

If you find typos in this book, they are there for a reason—
some people enjoy looking for them, and we strive to please as many readers as possible.

Table Of Contents

☞ These waterfalls may be more kid-friendly than others

Introduction

Welcome to my Arkansas Waterfalls Guidebook! If you have always been fascinated with falling water like I have, and want to get out and visit as many waterfalls as you can, or simply would like to go see a couple of the beautiful spots your friends have been telling you about, this is the book for you. If you are already a savvy outdoors person with years of backcountry experience, or have never set foot off the blacktop, there are waterfalls here for you. This guidebook will take you by the hand and lead you right to them.

Each waterfall listed includes a map that shows the parking area, suggested hiking route, the waterfall location, and other interesting features in the area. The text that goes with each map provides detailed directions about getting to the parking area, and how to get to the waterfall, whether it be along a well-used trail or road, or via a bushwhack through the backcountry. For those of you who like to take along the old standard USGS quad maps, the map name is listed. There is also a listing of the height of each waterfall, a beauty rating, length of hike required to reach the falls and get back to your vehicle, and a difficulty rating for that hike. Plus there is a black and white photo of each waterfall to give you an idea of what each looks like. And finally there is an emergency phone number listed at the end of each waterfall description.

Few people will be able to visit every waterfall in this guidebook (it took me several years to do so). Many of the waterfalls are located far back in the wilderness, with no trails in sight, and require not only experience and expertise to find, but also someone who is in very good physical condition and used to the hazards of backcountry travel. For those waterfalls I have provided bushwhacking route information, plus GPS coordinates for use in plotting the waterfall position on the map, as well as inputting into a GPS unit for use in navigation in the field. There are some real jewels out there that have seldom been visited, and if you have what it takes to get to them, you will be rewarded with some incredible sights.

Many of the waterfalls in this guidebook are either located right next to a road that you can drive to, or can be reached via a short, easy hike. In fact some of the most scenic waterfalls in the state are like this—Cedar Falls, Falling Water Falls, High Bank Twins, Triple Falls, Natural Dam, to name a few. Still others will require intermediate ability and navigational skills to reach, providing a bit of challenge for the casual hiker.

The waterfalls are divided into four different regions of the state where they are located—Buffalo River Drainage, the Ozarks outside of the Buffalo drainage, the Arkansas River Valley, and the Ouachitas. There is a location map at the beginning of each section, with the waterfall locations numbered on the map, and a listing of each waterfall corresponding to those numbers showing the details of each falls, along with the page number where the map and description can be found. There is an overall list of the waterfalls on the back cover with this same information, keyed to a state map inside the back cover.

Before you take off into the woods after any of these waterfalls I suggest that you read through the rest of this introduction. While it can never replace skills or conditioning, it will give you some basic knowledge needed to guide you through the use of this book, and enable you to get the most out of it. Read on!

MAPS Each of the maps in this guidebook was painstakingly researched, drawn by hand on a computer (that sounds odd but it's possible and true), then double and triple checked for accuracy. We started with regular USGS quads in the computer using software from MapTech (actual quad maps scanned to produce the software). Then we downloaded the GPS coordinates and track info that we gathered in the field (or should I say in the woods!) from the GPS unit to the computer, which then popped up on the quad maps. Next we printed out the quads with that info on them, drew in any additional information that we wanted, then scanned that into a second computer. My wife, Pam, took over at that point, and used a drawing program and drawing tablet with special pen to trace all of the pertinent information, creating the actual maps that are printed here. Then we added all of the stream names, road numbers, etc. to produce the final map.

There are no contour lines on the maps. I have always found that info to be much more than most folks care to deal with, and they really clutter up the map. If you enjoy and can appreciate contour maps, the USGS quad info is listed so that you will know which map to get, although none of the trails or waterfalls will be shown on them.

If you happen to find any mistakes on the maps (or in the text), please be sure to let us know so that we can correct them in future printings.

ROADS We are in a state of flux in Arkansas right now as far as road numbers and names are concerned. This has been a major headache for us as we have tried to compile and list all of the pertinent road numbers on the maps and in the text. One county just replaced all of its two-digit road numbers with four-digit numbers while we were putting this book together—we had to go back and change all of those numbers in this book. Some counties have multiple numbers for the same roads. Others have changed the road numbers to names. Some counties mark their roads quite well, while others don't have any markings whatsoever. And one county has only marked the roads on one side of the county and not the other! There are county roads that meander between two counties and either have a different number each time they enter a new county, or simply don't have a number or name at all. The old tried and true forest service road numbers are disappearing, being replaced by country or state numbers or names, but many of them are still in use and are marked that way. The bottom line is to go ahead and use the road names and numbers that we have listed here, but be aware that they are subject to change at any time.

You should be able to reach most of the parking areas noted in this guide with a regular vehicle. Some are reached via a jeep road and only accessible with a serious 4wd vehicle. You can still go visit the waterfall, but you might have to hike an extra mile or two to get there. Most of the time the description and hike length begin where a normal vehicle can reach—if you have a serious 4wd your hikes may be shorter, or not even necessary.

One precautionary note: you will often encounter thick fog on the highways in the early mornings and after rainstorms, so *slow down* and allow extra time to get there.

You can find a visual reference showing the different road types used on the maps on the map legend, which is located just inside the back cover. Since waterfalls tend to be located in the backcountry, it often requires a drive of several miles along gravel roads to reach the parking area. Forest roads are normally gravel and you can get most any vehicle down them, although in some cases they may be rough and you will need to drive slowly. Jeep roads normally require a high-clearance and/or 4wd vehicle to negotiate, although many of them are good enough that you can also get to the parking area with a regular vehicle—conditions change during the year, and from year to year, and often you will simply have to go have a look and see what the road looks like.

To simplify matters and save space I have shortened the road names to CR# (means County Road#) and FR# (means Forest Road#, sometimes signed as FS# on the ground).

The mileage to turnoffs and parking areas listed are the actual odometer readings from my vehicle. *I recommend that you use the trip counter in your vehicle religiously, and zero it often.* The mileages noted are often given in tenths, but keep in mind that these readings can vary from vehicle to vehicle greatly, and will depend on such factors as tire wear, road conditions and driving habits. So just like the road numbers, you should use the mileage figures as your guide, but be aware that they may differ a little bit from what is listed here. The maps/directions are from local points—be sure to bring a state highway map too!

PARKING AREAS Some of the waterfalls are located along well-used hiking or horse trails and have established and well-signed trailhead parking areas. Some waterfalls are located where there are no trails or official parking areas. Many times where you park will simply be where you can find enough room to pull off to the side of the road safely. Following the exact mileage readings and using a GPS will help you find the correct spot quicker. Other parking areas or trailheads may be noted on the maps (in black instead of red). Remote parking areas are no more susceptible to break-ins than any place, but it can happen anywhere, anytime. It's a good idea to hide your valuables or leave them at home.

HIKE DISTANCES AND DIFFICULTY The distance for hikes that is shown at the beginning of each waterfall listing is for a complete trip to the waterfall and back to the parking area. There is a running distance total in the description as well, marked at certain points along the way (in 0.0 miles unless otherwise noted). These distances were calculated using a variety of different methods, including rolling a measuring wheel over the ground, GPS distance readings, and careful plotting on the computer topo maps.

You will not see hiking *times* listed. The time it takes for you to reach a waterfall will depend on many factors, including your own personal hiking pace and style, weather conditions, what you see along the way to stop and look at, and especially how good a condition you are in. There is really no way for anyone to estimate how long it is going to take you to reach a certain point. Most people overestimate the time it takes for them to hike a mile, much less bushwhack through several miles of rugged terrain. My suggestion is to allow plenty of time—more than you would ever need. Then if you arrive at the waterfall early, that will give you ample time to enjoy the place, and have a leisurely hike back out.

The difficulty ratings at the front of each section and on the back cover are based on many factors, including length, type of terrain, and whether there is a trail or old road to hike on. The ratings are broken down further at the top of each individual waterfall listing to denote if it is a hike or bushwhack. A "hike" will be on an established trail or along an old road that is used as a trail. A "bushwhack" is when there is no trail or road to follow, and you simply are making your way through the woods. Bushwhacking is usually more difficult, time consuming, and requires a higher level of skill and expertise.

Easy Hike—short distance over generally level terrain following an established trail or road that most everyone should be able to make.

Medium Hike—longer distances of two or three miles up to eight or ten miles over varying terrain on established trails or roads. Most folks with hiking experience should be able to make these trips, although weaker hikers may have a tougher time.

Difficult Hike—longer distances of eight to ten miles or more over rough terrain but still following an established trail or road. Only those with a good bit of experience should attempt these.

Easy Bushwhack—short distance through the woods over easy terrain, no trail or road to follow. Most hikers should be able to make these trips as long as you are careful and watch where you are going, and how to get back!

Medium Bushwhack—longer distances of several miles or more over moderate terrain with some steep sections here and there, no trail or roads to follow. Experienced hikers who want a challenge can make these trips, but you need to be in good physical condition and have plenty of time, also be able to read a map well and/or use your GPS.

Difficult Bushwhack—longer distances of several miles or more over varying terrain that includes steep slopes, boulder scrambling, and fighting through thick brush. Only those with a great deal of experience in backcountry travel off trails who are in top physical condition and prepared for the rigors of serious bushwhacking should attempt these trips. A GPS is highly recommend, as well as a thorough knowledge of how to use it and read maps. You should also probably leave an updated will at home just in case.

WATERFALLS FOR KIDS! Few things will inspire a child more than a beautiful waterfall. Many of the falls in Arkansas are located in dangerous places along blufflines though, where one slip and something tragic could happen. Still, I feel like kids that are *older and can hike a few miles* need to get out and see waterfalls as they are growing up. My suggestion is for the parents to visit a waterfall first to see if it would be suitable for their own children. There are a number of waterfalls that may be more kid-friendly than others marked on the Table of Contents page. Most of them are either real easy to get to (some you can view from the car), and/or approach from the bottom of the falls so as not to be quite so dangerous. None of them are 100% safe, and parents still need to **hold on to** their kids at all times. Some of them require longer or steeper hikes—check them out first.

WATERFALL NAMES More than half of the waterfalls in this book did not have names until now, including some of the largest and most spectacular ones. The names for the classic waterfalls remain the same (with one exception—Twin Falls at Camp Orr is now referred to as Triple Falls). I used local names if I could find one. And if I came across a reference in a book, I used that name. But for all the rest of the waterfalls I had to simply make up names. I tried to see if there was a creek name or land formation that would fit (Dry Creek Falls, etc.). Or if something struck me about the falls while I was there (Paradise Falls, etc.). Finally, I wanted to honor many of the individuals who have contributed so much to the protection of wild places in Arkansas, or who have made other significant contributions (Neil Compton's Double Falls, Dale Bumpers Falls, etc.). A name becomes "official" when it is first published on a map or in a book—that's all there is to it.

The very first waterfall I ever named many years ago was Copperhead Falls, and that name has stuck. I have no idea if the names I have assigned to the waterfalls in this book will take or not, but I felt like I had to do something, otherwise there would be 75 or 80 "Unnamed" Falls in the listing and that wouldn't help much!

A "cascade" is just a waterfall that spills over many small ledges as opposed to one big leap, and the "run" can often be longer than the drop. A "pouroff" is where the water pours over a bluff that is flat across the top and has a straight edge in front, where a "falls" will normally have eroded a groove into the rock to some degree (many quite severe). All three names are interchangeable though (Cossatot Falls is really a long series of cascades).

BEAUTY RATING Yes, it is true that beauty is in the eye of the beholder and any beauty rating is purely subjective. So be it. I have tried to give you some idea of what I think about a particular waterfall in hopes of giving you an extra bit of information that might help you decide whether or not to visit that waterfall.

Often these ratings are not based solely on the waterfall itself— I also take into consideration the scenic value of the area surrounding the waterfall. For example, a 3-star waterfall might get bumped up to a 4-star or higher if there was a spectacular view at that spot, or if the falls was located in a really scenic canyon. It is the scenic *experience* that I am rating as much as the waterfall itself.

The height doesn't have all that much to do with the ratings—there are a number of 5-star falls that are less than 30 feet tall, and many 4-star falls that are more than 50 feet tall. In fact, many of the taller waterfalls are not all that interesting or scenic to me because the taller they are the narrower the waterfall appears—a similar flow on a shorter waterfall might be much more scenic.

And, of course, the beauty rating probably has more to do with the actual water level and flow on the day you visit than anything else. Many 4-star and 5-star waterfalls may only be rated as 3-star when water levels are low. Likewise, some 3-star falls may be 4-star or even 5-star falls if they were really cooking. Are you seeing stars yet?

WATERFALL HEIGHT The most commonly asked question about a waterfall is how tall it is. Many folks simply estimate the height of a falls and take it as gospel. I have always been a stickler for accuracy ever since my hunting buddy pulled out a weight scale and showed me that the "200 pound buck" I was bragging about was actually more like 95 pounds. Same thing with backpacks—how many people do you know who carry "an 80 pound backpack" into the woods? Most of those packs turn out to be 40 or 50 pounds. The simple fact is that most people cannot accurately estimate height. I went to great lengths (sorry about that pun) to measure almost every one of the waterfalls in this guidebook with a tape measure to get an accurate height (I have three different tapes, up to 300 feet long).

In some cases we had to bring in a rope team in order to get to the top of the falls with the tape measure. We did that with Hemmed-In Hollow, Diamond Falls, and Thunder Canyon. Many other falls had to be measured by two people since one person standing on top could not see the bottom of the falls and get an accurate measure—a second person on bottom placed the measuring tape where it needed to be. I would often have this second person guess the height of the waterfall before we measured it—and I would often guess myself. Then we would see how close we would get. Most guesses were way off, including mine. Only Glenn Wheeler, a former deputy sheriff, consistently came close to the actual measurement.

While I was writing this book (after all of the photos were shot and the information was gathered), I discovered a couple of waterfalls that I had not yet measured for one reason or another. So I made special trips out in the dead of summer, often requiring a half day or more trip for each, just to get an accurate measurement. Hey, I like accuracy.

Now, with all of the effort that we put into getting accurate measurements for this guidebook—sometimes literally risking life and limb to do so—I must tell you that a waterfall listed as 30 feet may only be 27 feet or may be 33 feet when you get there. Turns out there are many factors that contribute to the actual height, including the flow and volume of water going over the falls, and exactly where the top of the falls was measured from. High water volume often raises the height of the pool below, throwing off the mea-surement. Or the water may hit much farther down the slope when the water is running fast, sometimes adding 10 or more feet to the measurement.

As far as the actual *top* of the waterfall goes, that is really debatable. What I tried to find was the *visual* top of the waterfall, that is, what you can see from below. Often that meant including a short cascade that fed the very top of the waterfall. On the other hand, there are cases where part of the waterfall extended above what you could see from down below, and I normally included that additional height in the measurement. Sometimes the many drops of a waterfall were measured together, as in Lichen Falls, Twin Falls at Devil's Den, or Copperhead Falls—I consider all of the drops to be a single waterfall. If the drops were separated by much horizontal distance though, then I did not include the additional height in the measurement (I often listed them as two separate waterfalls, as in Bumpers Falls or McClure Falls). Some people will measure the height from the *bottom* of the top of the falls—getting only the actual vertical height of *free-fall,* but I really did not find that useful for my purposes (my kayaker friends live or *die* by that measurement!). So there you have it—now you can say with some authority that Hemmed-In Hollow Falls is offi-cially 209 feet tall and not 150 or 250 or 500 feet.

GPS Seems like everyone these days has a GPS unit that they take into the woods with them. Like topo maps, these things are a great help *if you know how to use them.* I still prefer to navigate "by the lay of the land" but do use a GPS more and more these days as a reference. They can be quite helpful when bushwhacking to a specific location, like a waterfall, especially if you have input the coordinates of the waterfall into your unit first. I also love to download the coordinates and tracks to my computer after a trip—it is al-ways fun to watch it all pop up on the monitor! If you are going to use GPS, I highly recommend that you have the topo software on your computer as well—that is when you will really get a great deal of use and pleasure out of the system. And I would make sure the topo software is *actual* USGS quad maps that have been scanned in and not the software developer's version of the topography (the software that we used while doing this book is Terrain Navigator by MapTech, which is what the search and rescue folks use).

There are coordinates for each waterfall listed above the individual maps, in two different formats—Digital Minutes (WGS 84) and UTM (NAD 27, all Zone 15S). These seem to be the two most commonly used formats, although most GPS units and computer programs are able to convert these numbers into other formats as well. I use these coordinates in my GPS unit and with the computer software, and seldom ever try to plot the location on an actual map, although I know others who swear by that method.

Speaking of putting things on the map, while GPS is certainly a wonderful tool and much more accurate these days then it used to be, using one won't always put you at the exact location where you want to be. If used properly, the GPS units will get you to within shouting distance of the waterfall, perhaps within a couple hundred feet, but don't count on hiking right to the very top of the falls instantly—you may have to look around a bit.

WATERFALL HUNTING SEASON The waterfalls in this guidebook will generally run to some degree much of the time in a normal year during "the wet season," which is late fall to early summer. Surface water normally will begin to flow once we get adequate rainfall after all of the leaves have fallen and the trees have gone dormant, usually late November. During the winter, once the ground is fully saturated, and early spring, most of the rain and snowfall runs off and produces great waterfalls—this is your prime waterfall viewing season. We seldom have a prolonged hard winter, and it is possible and quite enjoyable to get out and hike during the winter months. Of course, if we do have spells of freezing weather many of the waterfalls will produce spectacular ice displays! Once the trees begin to grow again in the springtime, they soak up billions of gallons of water a day, preventing rainfall from running off and feeding waterfalls. Fortunately, we typically have a lot of rain in the springtime, so the falls will continue to run until early summer when the rainfall simply will not keep up with the extreme demand of the forest. By June in a normal year things are drying up, and it takes a big rainfall to produce nice waterfalls.

You will not find waterfalls running during the summertime and early fall! Let me repeat—do not go looking for waterfalls in July, August, September, and October and expect to see them running! If you do you will be really disappointed. It certainly is possible though to have great waterfalls for short periods during this time. But it takes a great deal of rainfall over a period of days to get the ground fully saturated before waterfalls will run much. And even when they do, they won't run for very long.

The best time to go waterfall hunting is after it has rained for several days during the rainy season. If you go while it is still raining, you may see some incredible falls and cascades, but they often run muddy then, especially if it has been a hard rain. Often the creeks are swollen and running high with muddy water too—they are extremely dangerous to cross then and you may end up being swept away. *If you cannot see the bottom of the creek, do not cross it!*

Many of the photos in this guidebook were taken during periods of high water or even floods (noted below the photo). Most of the time these waterfalls will not look this good, even during the rainy season. In fact if we are having a dry year, or it has not rained in a week or two, you may find the waterfalls hardly running at all, even in the middle of the rainy season. The simple fact is that most of us do not have the luxury of taking off and heading into the woods during the optimum times—you have to take what you can get. I recommend that you take off as often as you can during the rainy season, and if the falls are not at their peak, I bet you enjoy a splendid hike to a beautiful area anyway!

WATERFALL PHOTOGRAPHY The key to getting great waterfall pictures is the quality of the light, pure and simple. Contrary to popular opinion, the best light for waterfalls is soft, diffused light, the kind that happens on overcast days. You can also take pictures very early or late in the day when the light is softer. If it is bright and sunny the light will be harsh and your pictures will not turn out as well.

The equipment that you use to take the pictures has much less to do with getting good pictures than does *how* you use your equipment. Here is the basic formula that I use for nearly every waterfall picture that I take, and will result in the water having that dreamy, silky look. Pick an overcast day. Use slow film (the faster the film speed, the *worse* the photos will be). Put your camera on a TRIPOD—this is an absolute must! Use a polarizing filter. If you have an adjustable camera, stop your lens down all the way. What you want is the longest exposure time that you can get—this will allow the moving water to be blurred on the film—you need an exposure of 1/2 second or longer to make that happen. (I typically have exposures in the 10–30 second range.) Use a cable release to trip the shutter if there is one available for your camera. And finally, take *lots* of pictures—move to different angles, change lenses, shoot vertically, and put someone in the photo for scale.

Most of the photos in this guidebook were taken with a digital camera (either 3 or 5 megapixel). Many of them were not only taken on overcast days, but often while it was raining, hard! I used an umbrella to keep the rain—and drips from blufflines overhead—off the camera. Keep your camera in a ziplock bag to help keep it dry.

I was solo when I took most of the pictures for this book, and always tried to get myself into the photo for scale. I would hit the self-timer and run/climb/scramble like crazy to get into the picture within the allotted ten seconds. And then I would have to hold perfectly still for several seconds during the exposure while I was breathing hard from the run. My wife, Pam, and friend, Glenn Wheeler, were brave enough to come along on many of the trips. Pam became a model for many of the photos, and took the pictures for others. Glenn is a photographer himself and snapped a lot of the photos.

AGENCY CONTACTS/PRIVATE LAND All but a few of the waterfalls in this guidebook are located on public land (noted on the maps). These lands belong to all of us, and are here for us to enjoy, as long as we take care of the land while we are doing it! For more info about these specific areas, contact the land managing agencies below. For free tourist and travel information, call 800–NATURAL. And for maps, guidebooks and other publications, call **800–838–HIKE,** or go to **www.HikeArkansas.com** (has links to everywhere).

Ozark National Forest	**Buffalo National River**	**Ouachita National Forest**
605 W. Main St.	402 N. Walnut St.	100 Reserve St.
Russellville, AR 72801	Harrison, AR 72601	Hot Springs, AR 71901
479–968–2354	870–741–5443	501–321–5202
Arkansas State Parks	**Arkansas Natural Heritage**	**Ark Game & Fish Comm**
One Capitol Mall	323 Center Street	#2 Natural Resources Dr.
Little Rock, AR 72201	Little Rock, AR 72201	Little Rock, AR 72205
501–682–1191	501–324–9619	501–223–6300

Several of the waterfalls are located on private land, and the landowners have granted permission for access to view them. Be sure to travel lightly when you visit, and leave no trace! (It was originally my intent to include only waterfalls on public land, but a few of these on private land slipped in.) There are many other beautiful waterfalls located on private lands that are not in this book—Bailey Falls, Bridal Veil Falls, Rainbow Falls, Hole In Rock Falls, and many others among them. Never trespass without permission!

THANK YOUS This was one of the toughest guidebooks I have ever done, and it would not have been possible without the help of the many great folks who were generous with their time and knowledge. I have been working on this project for many years and no doubt will fail to thank everyone. For those of you that I missed here, please forgive!

Neil Compton loved waterfalls, showed me many of the ones in this book, and is the one who first suggested that I write a guidebook to tell others about them. Terry Keefe is perhaps the state's leading waterfall guru now, and spent countless days in the woods taking me to waterfalls all over the map, and to several that were off of the map too! Another waterfall guru is Terry Fredrick, who spends more time out there chasing waterfalls than anyone I know. A giant thanks goes to Helen Elsner, who spends most of her time on horseback, and finds many great hidden scenic areas that she graciously shared with me (she wrote a neat book about the Buffalo River area). Others who either showed me individual waterfalls, sent me information about how to get to waterfalls, or helped out in some other way include: Jim McDaniel, Bill Herring, Brad Wimberly, Kevin Middleton, Steve Wilson (Game & Fish), Don Simons (Arkansas State Parks), Allen Twist, Mary Owen, T. Wayne Bailey, Danny Ruggles, Bob Wilson (Game & Fish), Les Claybrook (Game & Fish), Mark Hardgrave, Glenn Wheeler, Mike Mills, Steve Osborn (Forest Service), Rex & Gwen Benham, Lance Jones, Terry Hope (Forest Service), Michael Hughes, John Carroll, Bob Chester, Mary Woods, Keith Sutton (Game & Fish), Pledger Monk, Taos Jones, Ken Smith, Nancy Williams, Gene Boyd, Jeff Ash, Don Kurz, Duane Woltjen, Henry Robison, Joe Dempsey, Tari Underwood, Dale Oliver, Lee Roberts, Kris McMillen, John Vinson, Jim Steele (Forest Service), Paula White, Corbet Deary, and Dennis "Hete" Heter. Thanks to Russell & Yvonne Blaylock and Edd French for allowing public access to their land. Also a special thanks to Roy & Norma Senyard for their extra efforts to help measure some of the tougher falls. And thanks to Jason Swim from the Pack Rat Outdoor Center in Fayetteville for his GPS expertise. The text editors who did a great job to wade through all of my hillbilly speech and make it presentable were my lovely wife Pam, Norma Senyard, Sara Eisenbacher, and Judy Ferguson (Judy also came to our aid every time we yelled "It's raining, we've got to hit the road!" and filled in for us at the cabin). Glenn Wheeler helped in many ways, and took some of the photos. Thanks a second time to Pam, and to our daughter Amber—the only way that I am able to work on a project like this is to jump in head first and not surface until I am finished. Along the way I miss a lot of quality time that I should be spending with my family—for that I apologize, and thank you two immensely for putting up with me through it all! Finally, and for a third time, thanks to my bride for doing *so much work* on this project—she drew all of the maps, did research, edited text, spent a lot of time with me in dangerous situations in the woods, posed for photos, took photos, and never once recommended that I go see a shrink.

Now it is time to turn this guidebook and these waterfalls over to you, the future waterfall hunter, chaser, explorer. Go after each one with a twinkle in your eye and marvel at the incredible natural wonder that we have here in Arkansas, as I do still today each and every time that I come to a waterfall. And be careful as you go, to not only save your body for more excursions, but also to protect the fragile world that grows around waterfalls. It is up to you to insure that we have natural wonders to pass on for future generations.

Happy waterfall hunting!

Tim Ernst

Buffalo River Region Waterfalls

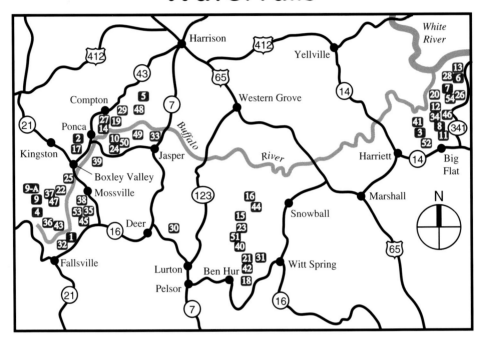

The Buffalo River region in northwest Arkansas is a land of towering limestone and standstone bluffs, caves, springs, rivers, and countless waterfalls. This section contains the waterfalls that are located in the actual watershed of the Buffalo River, which is one of the last free-flowing rivers in the United States. It has long been one of the premiere floating streams in the country, but once was threatened to be dammed up. The result of the long fight to save the Buffalo was the creation of America's first national river, Buffalo National River. Many of the waterfalls in this section are named after those individuals who led that fight. All of the waterfalls in this section are located in either the Buffalo National River or in the Ozark National Forest. There are still many great waterfalls out there that are not listed here—available for you to "discover" on your own! **NOTE:** dogs are not allowed on the trails within Buffalo National River (they are OK in the national *forest*).

Fall #	Name	Beauty Rating	Height	Hike Difficulty	Page #
1	Adkins Canyon Falls	★★★★★	42	Difficult	16
9-A	Amber Falls	★★★+	18	Medium	32
2	Armadillo Falls (2)	★★★★	18/24	Medium	42
3	Blow Cave Falls	★★★★	40	Easy	86
4	Bowers Hollow Falls	★★★★★	56	Difficult	20
5	Broadwater Hollow	★★★★	21	Easy	64
6	Bumpers Falls (2)	★★★★★	27/71	Easy	102
7	Cathedral Falls	★★★★★	87	Difficult	98
8	China Falls	★★★★+	68	Easy	88

Fall #	Name	Beauty Rating	Height	Hike Difficulty	Page #
9	Compton's Double Falls	★★★★★	39	Medium	32
10	Copperhead Falls	★★★★	13	Difficult	56
11	Cougar Falls	★★★★★	77	Easy	88
12	Crosscut Falls	★★★★+	53	Easy	88
13	Dewey Canyon Falls	★★★★★	88	Easy	102
14	Diamond Falls	★★★★★	148	Difficult	46
15	Dogwood Falls	★★★★	37	Medium	70
16	Dry Creek Falls	★★★★	20	Difficult	82
17	Eden Falls (4)	★★★★★	31-53	Easy	42
18	Falling Water Falls	★★★★	10	Easy	76
19	Fishtrap Hollow Falls	★★★★★	83	Difficult	50
20	Funnel Falls (2)	★★★★★	41/52	Medium	92
21	Fuzzybutt Falls	★★★★	16	Easy	78
22	Haley Falls (2)	★★★★	17/45	Medium	34
23	Hamilton Falls	★★★★	12	Difficult	72
24	Hammerschmidt Falls	★★★★+	43	Easy	54
25	Hedges Pouroff	★★★★★	113	Easy	38
26	Helen's Pouroff	★★★★★	71	Difficult	98
27	Hemmed-In Hollow	★★★★★	209	Difficult	46
28	Heuston Falls	★★★★+	54	Easy	102
29	Hideout Hollow Falls	★★★★+	37	Easy	52
30	Hudson Shelter Falls	★★★★	24	Easy	68
31	Keefe Falls	★★★★+	78	Medium	78
32	Leaning Log Falls	★★★★	27	Difficult	16
33	Liles Falls	★★★★	41	Easy	66
34	Little Glory Hole	★★★+	18	Easy	88
35	Magnolia Falls	★★★★	26	Medium	26
36	McClure Falls (2)	★★★★+	24/33	Difficult	22
37	Mule Trail Falls	★★★★	31	Medium	34
38	Paradise Falls	★★★★★	32	Difficult	30
39	Pearly Spring	★★★★★	34	Easy	40
40	Richland Falls	★★★★+	8	Difficult	72
41	Rory Ridge Falls	★★★★★	52	Easy	86
42	Six Finger Falls	★★★	6	Easy	78
43	Smith Falls (2)	★★★★★	54/71	Difficult	22
44	Stack Rock Homestead	★★★★	35	Easy	82
45	Stahle Falls	★★★★	63	Medium	26
46	Tassel Spring Falls	★★★+	44	Easy	96
47	Thousand Kisses Falls	★★★★	48	Medium	34
48	Thunder Canyon Falls	★★★★★	71	Medium	62
49	Triple Falls at Camp Orr	★★★★★	48	Easy	60
50	Tunnel Cave Falls	★★★★★	31	Difficult	56
51	Twin Falls at Richland Cr.	★★★★★	17/19	Difficult	72
52	Vickor Falls	★★★★	43	Easy	84
53	Woods Boys Falls	★★★★	33	Medium	26
54	Woodsman Pouroff	★★★★+	66	Difficult	98

Leaning Log Falls – ★★★★ – 27′

3.4 miles roundtrip, difficult bushwhack, GPS recommended
Lat/Lon–35 49.332 N, 93 25.617 W • UTM–4 **61** 448 E, 39 **64** 102 N, Fallsville Quad

Adkins Canyon Falls – ★★★★★ – 42′

Add .6 to above (4.0 total), difficult bushwhack, GPS recommended
Lat/Lon–35 49.393 N, 93 25.381 W • UTM–4 **61** 805 E, 39 **64** 214 N, Fallsville Quad

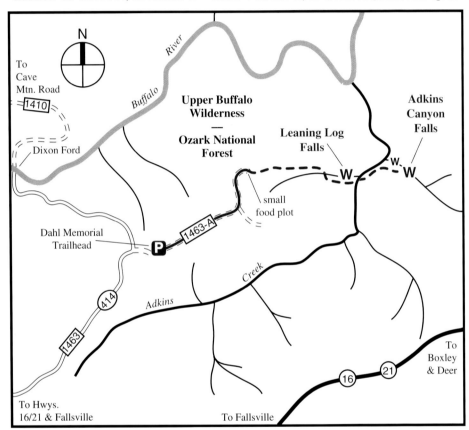

LEANING LOG FALLS/ADKINS CANYON FALLS. My first trip into this area was in 1979, right after a 10-inch snowfall had blanketed the area. I remember two things most about that trip: the fact that I did not carry a sleeping pad and had to sleep on a bed of snow; and these beautiful waterfalls that were covered with ice. I did not return to them until recently, and found them to be even more spectacular. The first part of the trip down into the canyon is an easy hike along a jeep road, but the second half of the trip involves some pretty serious bushwhacking, and the hike out is tough on a weary body.

From Fallsville take Hwy. 16/21 east for 1.4 miles and TURN LEFT onto FR#1463/CR#414. Go 2.0 miles and TURN RIGHT onto FR#1463–A and PARK at the Dahl Memorial Trailhead. (If you have a serious 4wd vehicle you can drive along the jeep road, but there are some big mud holes, and it's an easy hike, so best to park and hike.)

From the parking area head out to the east and hike along the jeep road there. It runs along the top of the ridge, dips down just a little bit, then back up again and levels off

Leaning Log Falls

where it comes to a "T" intersection at .8. TURN LEFT and continue to follow the jeep road as it makes its way on around the head of the hollow to the right and to a small food plot at 1.1. (This will be as far as you can go with a jeep—the wilderness boundary is just beyond.) I recommend that you begin to head down into the hollow to the right at this point, on an angle. When you come to the creek below TURN LEFT and follow the creek downstream. You will come to Leaning Log Falls at 1.7. There is a safe way to get down to the bottom of the falls after you cross the creek and go around to the right.

Lower Adkins Canyon Falls (upper falls is in background)

To get to Adkins Canyon from Leaning Log Falls go down to the river just below the falls—that is Adkins Creek. Find a way across it and follow it downstream to your LEFT. After a short distance you will come to a side drainage coming in from the right—that is the canyon, and you will see the lower waterfall right there. In fact it is a nice view from there looking up into the canyon because you can see all three waterfalls at the same time (see photo above). The lower two falls are not all that tall, but the entire little canyon area is really nice. You can find a route up the hill on the right side of the canyon and get to the upper Adkins Canyon Falls at 2.0.

Emergency contact: Newton County Sheriff, 870–446–5124

Upper Adkins Canyon Falls

Bowers Hollow Falls – ★★★★★ – 56′

4.0 miles roundtrip, difficult bushwhack, GPS highly recommended

Lat/Lon–35 51.257 N, 93 26.075 W • UTM–4 **60** 775 E, 39 **67** 665 N, Fallsville Quad

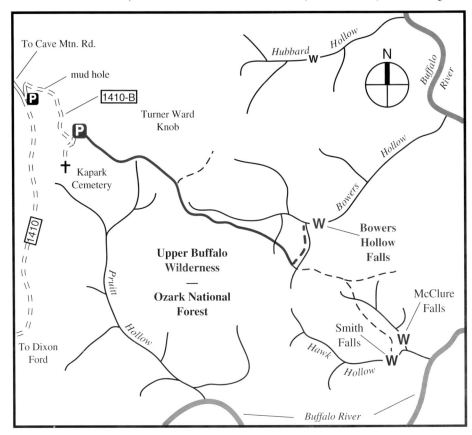

BOWERS HOLLOW FALLS. This is one of the most powerful and scenic waterfalls in Arkansas. The old road/trail into the area is used a lot by hikers so the path most of the way is easy to follow. The trail is not maintained, so there may be downed trees blocking the way. The last part is a steep bushwhack, and the falls will be easier to find with a GPS.

From Ponca, take Hwy. 43 south through Boxley to the intersection with Hwy. 21. TURN LEFT and follow Hwy. 21 for 1.2 miles (across two bridges) and TURN RIGHT just before you cross the bridge across the Buffalo River. This gravel road is Cave Mountain Road, and it takes off *steeply* up the hillside. Go past Cave Mtn. Church (at 5.5), Hawksbill Crag Trailhead (at 6.0), and TURN LEFT onto FR#1410 at 8.6. Go 1.6 miles and TURN LEFT onto FR#1410–B. If you have a normal car, PARK here (add 1.0 to your hike). If you have a 4wd you can continue on to the trailhead. The jeep road does continue on through a really bad mud hole for another .5 mile, then comes to a "T" intersection—TURN LEFT and PARK a few feet ahead where the road is blocked. (The other road goes to Kapark Cemetery.)

Begin hiking along the road past the hump. It is mostly level with a little bit of up and downing. At .8 you will come to a fork in the road, and may not even see it, but you want to TURN RIGHT and continue along the jeep road (be sure to make this turn on the way back out!). The road will now begin to drop on down the hill. At 1.2 you will come along-

Bowers Hollow Falls

side a creek on the left—it should be running well. This is the creek that runs through Bowers Hollow. You can simply follow that creek downstream until you come to the falls, or I recommend staying on the jeep road a little while longer and bushwhacking down the hill to the top of the falls. To do that, continue on the old jeep road as it remains fairly level but does a little up and downing as it crosses a couple of small creeks. At 1.7 you will come to a creek that is mostly filled up with wild rose bushes—look for a rock cairn (pile of rocks) on the left side of the road. TURN LEFT at the creek and follow it down the hill and you will come out right at the top of the falls at 2.0. It is indeed a magical spot—enjoy!

Emergency contact: Newton County Sheriff, 870–446–5124

Smith Falls (2) – ★★★★★ – 54'/71'

5.4 miles roundtrip, difficult hike/bushwhack, GPS highly recommended
Lat/Lon–35 50.625 N, 93 25.569 W • UTM–4 **61** 532 E, 39 **66** 492 N, Fallsville Quad

McClure Falls (2) – ★★★★+ – 24'/33'

Same area as above, difficult hike/bushwhack, GPS highly recommended
Lat/Lon–35 50.730 N, 93 25.541 W • UTM–4 **61** 574 E, 39 **66** 687 N, Fallsville Quad

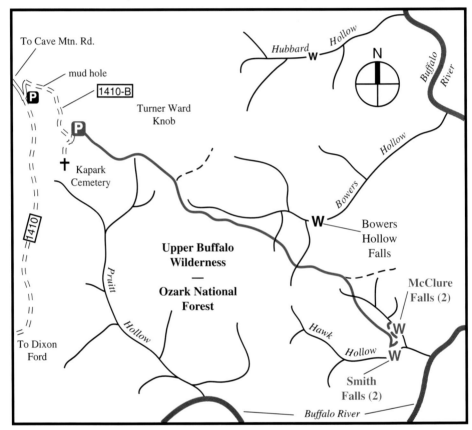

SMITH FALLS/McCLURE FALLS. I first found out about this little scenic area that contains these four waterfalls from Ken Smith, who had spent a great deal of time exploring these hills in the early 1960's. The forest service had originally wanted to protect only 625 acres of this "scenic area." The wilderness is now more than 13,000 acres. Ken worked tirelessly for many years with Neil Compton and the Ozark Society to get the Buffalo River area protected. It is fitting that two of the most beautiful waterfalls now bear his name.

Two others that were inspired by Ken Smith in the years to come were Tom McClure and Ellen Neaville. Tom led the fight for the Arkansas Wilderness Coalition in the early 1980's that resulted in the creation of most of the wilderness areas we have in Arkansas. When a group of us traveled to Washington, D.C. to testify before Congress about wilderness, Tom and I bunked together. I found it funny when he came knocking on my door in the middle of the night wanting to know if I had a spare toothbrush—he is a *dentist*, but had forgotten his! Ellen worked on the wilderness campaign, and was also instrumental in

Upper Ken Smith Falls

creating many of the "Natural Areas" that we have in Arkansas through the Natural Heritage Commission. Most importantly though, she has devoted her life to educating our young people about the natural world, and the creatures and plants that call it home. In a wonderful twist of fate these two people so dedicated to the environment recently got married. The waters of the pair of McClure Falls flow together as one.

The access for these waterfalls is the same as for Bowers Hollow Falls, and the first 1.7 miles of the route into them is the same as well. See the previous two pages for the directions to the trailhead, and for the first 1.7 miles of trail.

Once you get to the 1.7 mile point on the hike into Bowers Falls—at the point where you leave the road and bushwhack down to the falls—CONTINUE STRAIGHT AHEAD to get to Smith/McClure Falls. Stay on the road trace as it levels out and passes through an area with lots of giant trees around. Many of the trees were knocked down by a tornado that swept through the area in the late 1990's. At 2.0 the road will make a turn

Lower Ken Smith Falls

to the left—look for a rock cairn on the RIGHT, where a smaller old road trace takes off—TURN TO THE RIGHT (straight ahead) and go down the hill on the smaller road.

Follow this little road down the hill and across a small stream, then along a level bench just up above the stream, which will be down on your left. The road remains basically level as it curves on around the nose of a ridge to the right. As you come around the hill and straighten out look for a trail that leaves the road and goes down the hill TO THE LEFT. This little trail will take you right on down to the top of the Upper Smith Falls, which will be on the left at 2.7. The unofficial name for this area is Hawk Hollow.

To get to McClure Falls from the top of Smith Falls, follow the top of the bluff to the left, past the overhang *(careful!)*, and on around the mountain and you will come to McClure Falls on the right. It is possible to get down below the bluffline to both Lower McClure and Lower Smith Falls by going on around the bluff beyond McClure Falls 100 yards or so, but the trip down into that area is *very steep and hazardous,* and only for experts.

Emergency contact: Newton County Sheriff, 870–446–5124

Upper McClure Falls

Lower McClure Falls

Magnolia Falls – ★★★★ – 26′

2.1 miles roundtrip, medium hike/bushwhack, GPS recommended
Lat/Lon–35 51.923 N, 93 23.904 W • UTM–4 **64** 047 E, 39 **68** 882 N, Fallsville Quad

Woods Boys Falls – ★★★★ – 33′

Same location as above, medium hike/bushwhack, GPS recommended
Lat/Lon–35 51.936 N, 93 23.942 W • UTM–4 **63** 991 E, 39 **68** 906 N, Fallsville Quad

Stahle Falls – ★★★★ – 63′

Add .6 mile to above , medium hike/bushwhack, GPS recommended
Lat/Lon–35 51.919 N, 93 24.114 W • UTM–4 **63** 731 E, 39 **68** 876 N, Fallsville Quad

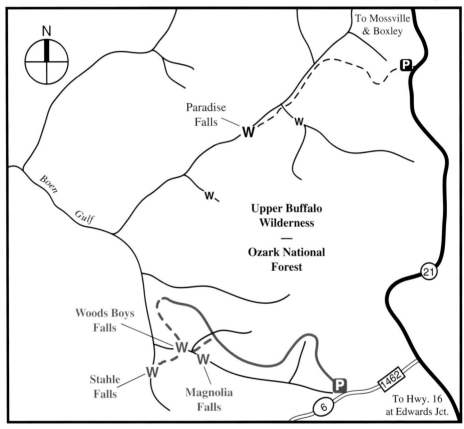

MAGNOLIA/WOODS BOYS/STAHLE FALLS. For the amount of effort involved to reach these waterfalls, getting to see all three in the same trip is a pretty good bang for your buck. The hike is mostly on an old jeep road, and the scenery is first rate.

The turnoff for the trailhead is located between Mossville and Edwards Junction on Hwy. 21. From the Mossville Church go south on Hwy. 21 for 2.5 miles and TURN RIGHT onto FR#1462/CR#6 (gravel—may not be marked); OR go north on Hwy. 21 from Edwards Junction for 1.8 miles and TURN LEFT onto the gravel road. Go just .3 mile on the gravel road and PARK on the right at the "Wilderness Access" sign.

From the main gravel road hike on the jeep road past some mud holes, to the trailhead

Magnolia Falls

register just down the road. CONTINUE STRAIGHT AHEAD here along the road trace. You'll cross a small creek and then come to an intersection of sorts about 100 yards beyond—TURN LEFT onto a jeep road as you enter the wilderness boundary (painted blue blazes on the trees).

This little road drops on down the hill past some interesting stone walls and rock formations up on the right. After you have gone just about 1.0 mile, the road will dip down and come to a little creek, then the road heads uphill just a little bit. You want to TURN LEFT at the creek and follow it downstream, leaving the road. This creek will take you on down just a couple hundred yards to a larger creek below. Magnolia Falls will be just upstream on the larger creek, and Woods Boys Falls will be just downstream.

From here you will have a couple of options. If you simply want to make an easy hike on over to see Stahle Falls from the top, make your way on around and up to the top of Magnolia Falls and cross the creek up there, then follow the top of the bluffline on around

Woods Boys Falls

to the right until you come to the falls. This area is thick with huckleberry underfoot.

If you want a longer (add 2.0 miles to the roundtrip total), more scenic hike, then back up and return to the jeep road at the point where you left it. CONTINUE hiking along the road. It will bump up just a little, then drop on down the hill at a pretty good clip, coming underneath some overhanging bluffs. At the bottom of those bluffs TURN LEFT and bush-whack along the base of that bluffline to the bottom of Woods Boys Falls.

The Woods Boys are Danny, Billy, Spanky, Kenny, and Landon Woods, all friends of mine who grew up in the area and probably know this country better than anyone. They logged the forest by hand, and took very good care of it in the process.

Dave Stahle Falls (the top of the falls is out of sight)

From Woods Boys Falls continue following the base of the bluff to the right and you will eventually come to the bottom of Stahle Falls. Professor Dave Stahle is another friend of mine, and owns a cabin at the head of this drainage. He is one of the world's leading authorities on determining the age of trees. There are some in this area many hundreds of years old. He can bore into a tree and show you evidence of great floods, fires and drought.

The entire Boen Gulf drainage is filled with boulders and cascades and great scenery. Take care as you travel and be good to the land, just like the Woods family has been doing here for generations.

Emergency contact: Newton County Sheriff, 870–446–5124

Paradise Falls – ★★★★★ – 32′

2.4 miles roundtrip, difficult bushwhack, GPS recommended

Lat/Lon–35 52.871 N, 93 23.586 W • UTM–4 **64** 533 E, 39 **70** 632 N, Boxley Quad

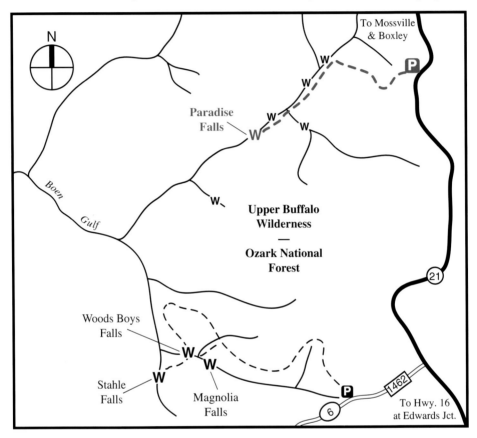

PARADISE FALLS. Something about this falls made me think of a tropical paradise the minute I saw it. It's a wide cascade that plunges down into a large emerald pool. I happened upon it one day while simply out exploring some drainages to see what I could find. Seems like a perfect skinny-dipping hole to me!

There is no trail but part of the hike is along an old logging road, and there are several smaller waterfalls along the way. To get to the parking spot, take Hwy. 21 south from the Mossville Church (between Boxley and Edwards Junction). Go just .8 mile and PARK on the right at a pulloff area. (OR 3.4 miles north on Hwy. 21 from Edwards Junction) There is an old road that is closed and blocked that takes off to the west from this spot.

Hike along the old road as it heads down a hill. It will soon level out some and come to an intersection—there are a number of logging roads in this area—all of them growing up—and things will be rather confusing, but as long as you keep going downhill you will eventually get to the waterfall. A GPS will help. At the first intersection stay STRAIGHT AHEAD and curve a little to the left. Soon you will come to an area where there are several old roads that take off—TURN RIGHT and head straight down the hill on one of the road traces. Continue on down the hill past a couple of more intersections, and eventually you will curve around to the right and enter the wilderness boundary (blue blazes on

Paradise Falls

the trees). If you are at the right spot, the old road will cross a creek not too far beyond the boundary paint at about .6. There is a small waterfall on the creek just below where the old road crosses the creek. TURN LEFT and bushwhack down alongside the creek.

You will pass another waterfall and then a good-sized creek coming in from the left at 1.0 (there is a nice waterfall just upstream to the left on that creek). CONTINUE STRAIGHT AHEAD and downstream. If the water is running high you will probably have to be up on the hillside looking down on the creek instead of right alongside it. You will pass another waterfall and cascade area, and then you will come to the top of Paradise Falls at 1.2.

If you are a tough woodsman and have lots of time and energy, it is possible to find your way downstream and then back up a different fork of Boen Gulf to the trio of waterfalls noted on the bottom of this map and described on the previous pages.

Emergency contact: Newton County Sheriff, 870–446–5124

Compton's Double Falls – ★★★★★ – 39'

2.1 miles roundtrip, medium bushwhack, GPS helpful

Lat/Lon–35 52.758 N, 93 27.754 W • UTM–4 **58** 262 E, 39 **70** 450 N, Boxley Quad

Amber Falls – ★★★+ – 18'

.7 miles roundtrip, medium bushwhack, GPS helpful

Lat/Lon–35 53.037 N, 93 28.210 W • UTM–4 **57** 578 E, 39 **70** 970 N, Boxley Quad

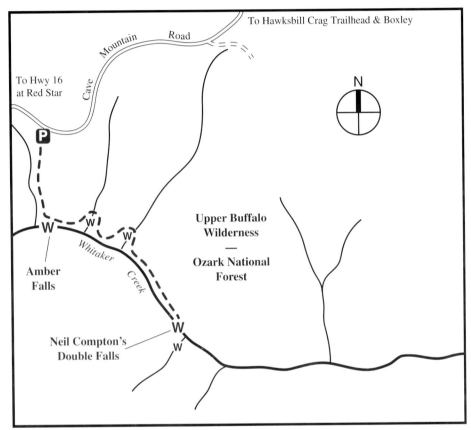

NEIL COMPTON'S DOUBLE FALLS/AMBER FALLS. Neil Compton sat on our deck at Cloudland one morning and told about the cougar scat he had found just above this water-fall many years before. No one could tell a story like Neil Compton, and he made the simple act of finding a pile of scat seem extraordinary. No one has done more for the natural beauty of Arkansas than he. The day he died I decided to name this beautiful double waterfall in his honor—no single falls would do. His vision is what saved the Buffalo River, and is why so many of us attempt to follow his path and keep the torch lit to protect our wild places. That cougar is out there somewhere, keeping Neil's spirit alive.

Neil enjoyed taking kids into the wilderness, and he would have approved of me naming a waterfall just upstream from his after my own daugher, Amber. She is a special young lady and loves the outdoors. The photo of her waterfall is on page 223.

There is no trail to these falls, but it is a simple bushwhack to get down to them (not so easy coming back out!). The parkingspot is located on Cave Mountain Road near the Hawksbill Crag Trailhead. From Ponca take Hwy. 43 south through Boxley Valley to the

Neil Compton's Double Falls (during *very* high water)

intersection with Hwy. 21. TURN LEFT and go south on Hwy. 21 for 1.2 miles (over two bridges) and TURN RIGHT onto Cave Mtn. Road (gravel) just before the bridge over the Buffalo River (zero your odometer). This road is *steep!* You will pass Cave Mtn. Church at 5.4, then the Hawksbill Crag Trailhead at 6.0. CONTINUE PAST the trailhead for another 1.1 miles until you come to a wooden sign on the left that says "Upper Buffalo Wilderness" and PARK along the road (there are actually two signs near each other there).

Head into the woods behind the sign and bushwhack *straight down* the hill. There is a small drainage on the right—follow this all the way to the bottom of the hill where you will hit Whitaker Creek (there is an old roadbed part of the way). Once you get to the bottom, TURN LEFT and follow Whitaker Creek downstream. You will come to Amber Falls almost immediately.

To get to Compton's Falls from there continue heading downstream—stay up on the bench overlooking the creek, keeping Whitaker Creek just off to your right. You will pass a couple of other nice waterfalls that come in on side drainages along the way. You will know Neil's waterfall when you come to it—the the creek will drop away sharply below, and you will hear a big roar. It takes a good bit of water to get this waterfall running as a double, so save it for a rainy day! Hike back out the same way that you came in.

Emergency contact: Newton County Sheriff, 870–446–5124

Haley Falls (2) – ★★★★ – 17'/45'

2.2 miles roundtrip, medium hike, GPS not needed
Lat/Lon–35 53.610 N, 93 26.813 W • UTM–4 **59** 685 E, 39 **72** 020 N, Boxley Quad

Mule Trail Falls – ★★★★ – 31'

2.2 miles roundtrip (inc. above), medium hike/bushwhack, GPS helpful
Lat/Lon–35 53.618 N, 93 26.993 W • UTM–4 **59** 414 E, 39 **72** 034 N, Boxley Quad

Thousand Kisses Falls – ★★★★ – 48'

Add .2 to above, medium hike/bushwhack, GPS helpful
Lat/Lon–35 53.545 N, 93 27.032 W • UTM–4 **59** 354 E, 39 **71** 901 N, Boxley Quad

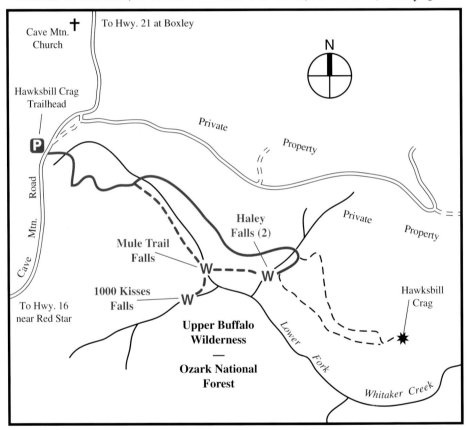

HALEY/MULE TRAIL/THOUSAND KISSES FALLS. The largest search and rescue mission in Arkansas history centered around Haley Falls, and was the subject of a ***Dateline NBC*** story, my book ***The Search For Haley***, and countless other media reports. Six-year-old Haley Zega got separated from her group and was on her own in the wilderness for three days and two nights—all she wanted was to go have a closer look at the waterfall that would later bear her name. Haley Falls is located along the trail to the famous Hawksbill Crag. The other two falls are in the same area, but require a bit of bushwhacking to find.

The trailhead is located just off Cave Mountain Road near the Hawksbill Crag Trailhead. From Ponca take Hwy. 43 south through Boxley Valley to the intersection with

Lower Haley Falls (during high water)

Hwy. 21. TURN LEFT and go south on Hwy. 21 for 1.2 miles (over two bridges) and TURN RIGHT onto Cave Mtn. Road (gravel) just before the bridge over the Buffalo River (zero your odometer). The road goes *steeply* up Cave Mountain. You will pass Cave Mountain Church at 5.4, and come to the Hawksbill Crag Trailhead at 6.0—PARK there.

We are going to do a loop to visit all three waterfalls, but you could cut the trip short and only see two of them if you wanted, or just see Haley Falls and come back. The trail begins across the road from the parking lot and drops down a rocky slope, across a tiny stream (if it is running, there will be water in Mule Trail Falls!), and up a rise to the trailhead register. The trail switchbacks down the hill and comes to the creek again at .4. (If you only wanted to visit Mule Trail and Thousand Kisses, turn right and follow this creek downstream .4 to Mule Trail, then follow the bluff to the right to Thousand Kisses.)

From the creek crossing the main trail remains level for a while, then drops on down a bench and comes to a larger creek at 1.0 and a trail intersection. The trail to the left is the upper route to Hawksbill Crag. You want to TURN RIGHT and follow the creek down-

35

Mule Trail Falls (above), **Upper Haley Falls** (below—during high water)

Thousand Kisses Falls (during high water)

stream 100 yards and you will come to the Upper Haley Falls (this is where Haley got lost).

If you are careful it is possible to find a way down this upper bluffline over on the left side, and get to the base of the upper falls. From there go behind the upper falls and you can get down to the base of the lower falls from over on the right side of them.

To continue with the hike follow along the base of the bluffline to the northwest (to your LEFT as you are looking up at the falls) and you will come to Mule Trail Falls at 1.4. There is an old mule trail there that once ran all the way up from the mouth of Whitaker Creek on the Buffalo River to Cave Mountain Road (much of this route has disappeared).

From this falls continue along the bluffline (either above or below) and you will come to Thousand Kisses Falls at 1.5. When I first took my bride-to-be Pam here I promised that I would kiss her under 1,000 more waterfalls in our lifetime together. I've got a long ways to go, but look forward to each and every one of them!

To get back to the trailhead return to Mule Trail Falls and follow the creek there upstream until you intersect with the main trail—TURN LEFT and follow the trail back to the trailhead. This creek is the Lower Fork of Whitaker Creek.

Emergency contact: Newton County Sheriff, 870–446–5124

Hedges Pouroff – ★★★★★ – 113′

400 yards roundtrip, easy bushwhack, GPS not needed

Lat/Lon–35 56.697 N, 93 25.023 W • UTM–4 **62** 401 E, 39 **77** 713 N, Boxley Quad

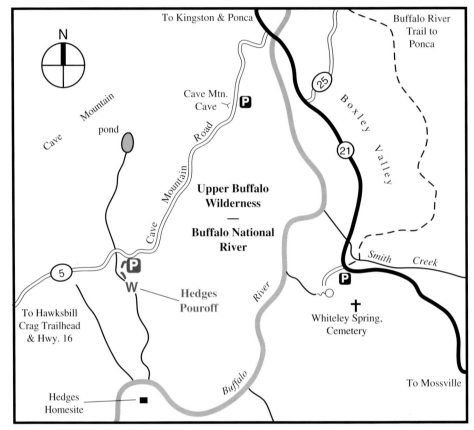

HEDGES POUROFF. I drove past the little creek that forms this waterfall hundreds of times, always thinking, "There must be a waterfall down there somewhere!" One day I finally stopped and took a look. Not only did I find one of the tallest waterfalls in Arkansas, but also one incredible view as well—one of the best in all the Buffalo region. This pouroff is named after Harold and Margaret Hedges who had a beautiful home down in the valley along the river. They could look up and marvel at this falls from their front porch. Harold once told me he had seen as many as *nine* waterfalls coming off this spot at the same time! (It wasn't moonshine he had been drinking, but rather the fact that the creek splits up as it gets to the top of the bluff, and the more water there is, the more waterfalls it creates.) They were instrumental in helping to get the Buffalo saved as a National River, and we all owe them a great deal. Their lovely home was burned to the ground one year while they were away for Christmas, and it is widely believed it was an act of arson by people opposed to the river being protected. The home was never rebuilt.

To get to the parking area you need to find Cave Mountain Road. Take Hwy. 43 south from Ponca through Boxley Valley to the intersection with Hwy. 21. TURN LEFT onto Hwy. 21 there and go 1.2 miles (over two bridges) and TURN RIGHT just before you cross over the Buffalo River bridge. This is Cave Mountain Road (gravel) and it probably

Hedges Pouroff

will not be marked, although there will be several mailboxes there. Follow this road as it climbs *steeply up* Cave Mountain. Go 1.4 miles (almost 1.5) and find a place to PARK on the LEFT. This will be a couple of hundred yards after you climb up through the bluffline and level out on top. You will be able to look out to your left and see that you are up high. If you come to the little creek that flows under the road, go back 100 yards and park.

Hike down the slope from the road until you reach the top of the bluff, then TURN RIGHT until you come to the falls. OR simply follow the little creek down to the falls. It is only 200 yards or less. The main falls pours out from under an ancient cedar tree that is growing over the edge, and then the water crashes onto the jagged rocks far below. It is a difficult falls to photograph. This is a 100 foot tall bluff so ***extreme caution is advised!!!***

Emergency contact: Newton County Sheriff, 870–446–5124

Pearly Spring – ★★★★★ – 34′
200 yards roundtrip, easy hike, GPS not needed
Lat/Lon–36 00.071 N, 93 22.133 W • UTM–4 **66** 768 E, 39 **83** 933 N, Ponca Quad

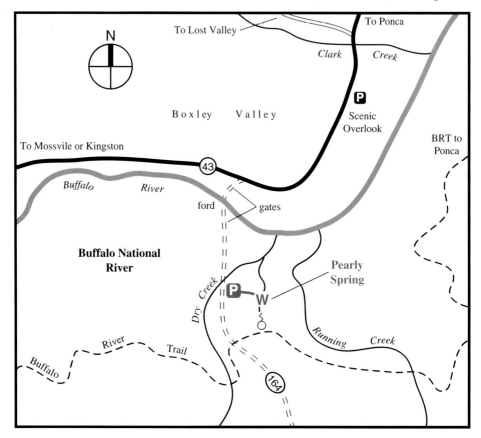

PEARLY SPRING. I took a picture of this spring one time and got paid 300 bottles of beer for it (the photo was used as the label on Arkansas Ale). The falls are down below the actual spring, and you can often find the falls running to some degree when the other waterfalls are low. This has always been a cool, refreshing spot, and the rocks around the bottom are covered with bright-green moss.

There are two ways to get to the parking spot. The first one is accessible only when the Buffalo River is low enough to drive/hike across. The turnoff is located in Boxley Valley, just south of Ponca on Hwy. 23—go .2 past the turnoff into Lost Valley (just past the so-called "scenic" pullout) and TURN LEFT onto a hidden drive (dirt) that goes steeply down the hill to a gate. If the gate is closed it is OK to open and go through it, but make sure that you close it *immediately* behind you! This jeep road fords the Buffalo River just beyond, goes through a second gate, and crosses Dry Creek. PARK where you can just after the creek crossing and before the jeep road begins to head up the hill.

When the river is high take the long route, which is via a rough county road from above. From Low Gap on Hwy. 74 between Ponca and Jasper, take CR#24 (paved at first, but turns to gravel up on top of the hill). Go 3.9 miles and TURN RIGHT onto CR#164 (gravel). You will think that this road is taking you to the very edge of the earth, but stick

Pearly Spring

with it. After about 7.0 miles the road has dropped down the hill, crossed the Buffalo River Trail, and bottomed out—PARK where you can just before crossing Dry Creek (the Buffalo River is just ahead). NOTE that this area is a working farm—no camping.

Hike from the gravel road to the east along a little road trace to a stream about 100 yards from where you parked—the waterfall below the spring is just up to your RIGHT. Be careful not to step on any of the moss-covered rocks.

Emergency contact: Newton County Sheriff, 870–446–5124

Eden Falls (4) – ★★★★★ – 31'-53'

2.3 miles roundtrip, easy hike, GPS not needed

Lat/Lon–36 01.051 N, 93 23.238 W • UTM–4 **65** 117 E, 39 **85** 751 N, Osage SW Quad

Armadillo Falls (2) – ★★★★ – 18'/24'

Add .4 to above, easy bushwhack, GPS helpful

Lat/Lon–36 00.909 N, 93 22.853 W • UTM–4 **65** 693 E, 39 **85** 486 N, Osage SW Quad

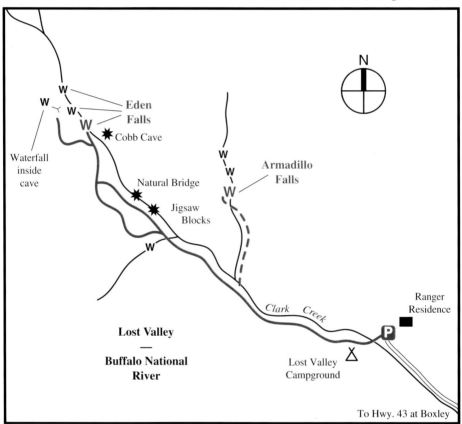

EDEN FALLS/ARMADILLO FALLS. Lost Valley is one of the crown jewels of the Ozarks, and Eden Falls one of the most beautiful, and most visited waterfalls in the region. It's easy to get to, even for kids and older folks. There are actually four separate waterfalls there, including one back inside a cave (take a flashlight). And if you are in the mood for a bit of bushwhacking, there are several more falls off in a side canyon that we'll visit. *No dogs.*

Lost Valley is easy to find—the turnoff is just south of Ponca on Hwy. 43. Follow the gravel road back to the primitive campground area and PARK. The trail heads off across a bridge over Clark Creek. While more water makes it better, you *may* still see a good water-fall even if Clark Creek is dry at the bridge (the water often goes underground). Follow the trail upstream to .7 and take the RIGHT fork—past the Jigsaw Blocks and the Natural Bridge (a small waterfall exits this tunnel). The trail climbs up next to the creek and rejoins the main trail—TURN RIGHT and follow it on over to Cobb Cave and to the base of Lower Eden Falls at 1.1. This is the falls that most people see. Continue on up the trail (steep) and it will

Lower Eden Falls

end at the mouth of Eden Falls Cave. Middle Eden Falls just below is created by the stream that exits the cave (turn page for photo). You can get a glimpse of Upper Eden Falls in the gorge upstream (turn page for photo). The waterfall in the cave is located just a couple hundred feet inside—it pours out of the ceiling 30 feet above you (turn page for photo).

On the way back out, locate the stream coming in from the opposite side of the valley on the left, go across Clark Creek, and follow this side creek upstream a couple of hundred yards to the base of Armadillo Falls (not suitable for small kids). At one point you can see three different waterfalls at the same time—the upper one is the tallest, but out of reach.

Emergency contact: Newton County Sheriff, 870–446–5124

**Upper
Eden Falls**

**Waterfall *inside*
Eden Falls Cave**
(above, w/natural
lighting)

**Middle
Eden Falls**

**Middle
Armadillo Falls**

**Lower
Armadillo Falls**

Hemmed-In Hollow Falls – ★★★★★ – 209′

5.0 miles roundtrip, difficult hike, GPS not needed
Lat/Lon–36 04.328 N, 93 18.452 W • UTM–4 **72** 323 E, 39 **91** 784 N, Ponca Quad

Diamond Falls – ★★★★★ – 148′

Add .5 to above, difficult bushwhack, GPS not needed
Lat/Lon–36 04.300 N, 93 18.568 W • UTM–4 **72** 148 E, 39 **91** 733 N, Ponca Quad

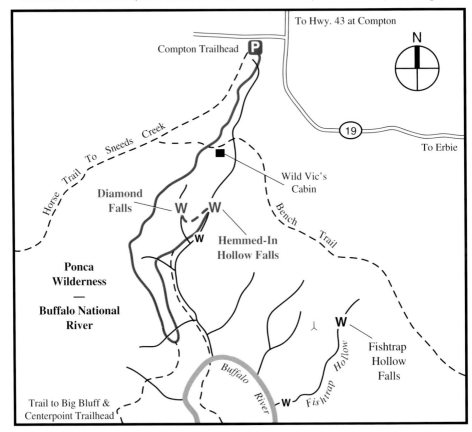

HEMMED-IN HOLLOW FALLS/DIAMOND FALLS. Hemmed-In Hollow Falls is the tallest waterfall between the Appalachians and the Rockies. Many thousands of folks have seen it, and it continues to be one of the most popular destinations in the Ozarks. What a lot of folks don't realize is that the second tallest waterfall in Arkansas—Diamond Falls— is literally just right around the corner. You can get to both falls by making the short hike up from the river if you are floating the Buffalo from Steele Creek to Kyles. You can also hike the trail down from Center Point (past Big Bluff and Granny Henderson's Cabin). But a quicker way to the falls is from the Compton Trailhead, and that is what we are going to do. NOTE that while the total hike miles may seem short on paper, the trail is *steep and rugged,* and the climb out is *more than a thousand feet __up__*—you should be in great shape for this one, and plan an entire day for the hike! *No dogs allowed on the trail.*

The turnoff for the trailhead is located at Compton, between Harrison and Ponca on Hwy. 43. Take the gravel road across from the post office in Compton (CR#19), TURN

Hemmed-In Hollow Falls

RIGHT at the first intersection, and go just less than a mile and TURN RIGHT into the trailhead parking lot. There are two trails that leave this lot—the one on the right is a horse trail that goes down to Sneeds Creek and beyond. For a longer hike you can return on this trail and make a 7.2 mile loop.

Hike down the trail on the left, and follow it across a small stream (this feeds Hemmed-In Hollow Falls) and then on down the rocky hillside. You will come to a trail intersection at .7—GO STRAIGHT THERE. (The trail to the left is the Bench Trail that you take to get

Twin falls below Hemmed-In Hollow (during high water)

to Fishtrap Hollow Falls—the directions to it follow this entry—and the trail to the right connects with the horse trail to Sneeds Creek.) Wild Vic's Cabin is located down the trail to the left several hundred yards, and makes for an interesting side trip.

From the trail intersection our trail continues heading down the hillside, and it gets pretty steep at times. There is a terrific viewpoint at 1.5—you can look over to your left and see Hemmed-In Hollow Falls, and out to the right is the Buffalo River and the wilderness beyond. Continue down the steep trail until you come to another intersection at 1.8. TURN LEFT there. The trail to the right goes out to Granny's Cabin, Big Bluff and to the Center Point Trailhead, and connects with the horse trail that runs up Sneeds Creek and on back out to our trailhead.

OK, so turn left at that intersection. You are now heading up into Hemmed-In Hollow proper, hiking through a wonderful beech forest. You will drop down and cross a creek at 2.2, and just beyond intersect with the trail that goes down the hollow to the Buffalo River—continue STRAIGHT AHEAD there. Hemmed-In Hollow Creek is now down to your right, and soon you will come to and cross another creek that flows right into it. The photo above was taken at the junction of the two creeks.

The trail continues up the main creek, past another waterfall down on your right. Then the trail intersects with the creek itself, and you will have to cross it. Once you do, you will be standing at the base of Hemmed-In Hollow Falls at 2.5. If it is a windy day, the falls will be tossed back and forth by the wind. It is truly one of the greatest natural spots in mid-America. The photo on the previous page was shot from the side and does not include the entire falls—note the second guy in the photo for scale.

Diamond Falls is located to the left of Hemmed-In Hollow Falls, and around the corner, but to get to it you have to first climb up to the right of the big falls, and go behind them.

Diamond Falls

Continue making your way across the bluffline behind the falls and out the other end—there are several ancient, twisted and weathered cedar trees there. Just keep going on around at the base of this bluffline to the left, and you will come to Diamond Falls within a quarter mile. Neil Compton named it Diamond Falls because the big plunge often hits a rock shelf part way down, sending spray all over the place. When backlit by the sun high above it looks like a million diamonds falling from the sky. This is a tough waterfall to photograph—the spray gets you when you're up close, and trees fill the frame if you back off.

Emergency contact: Newton County Sheriff, 870–446–5124

Fishtrap Hollow Falls – ★★★★★ – 83′

4.2 miles roundtrip, difficult bushwhack, GPS highly recommended

Lat/Lon–36 03.897 N, 93 17.932 W • UTM–4 **73** 101 E, 39 **90** 983 N, Ponca Quad

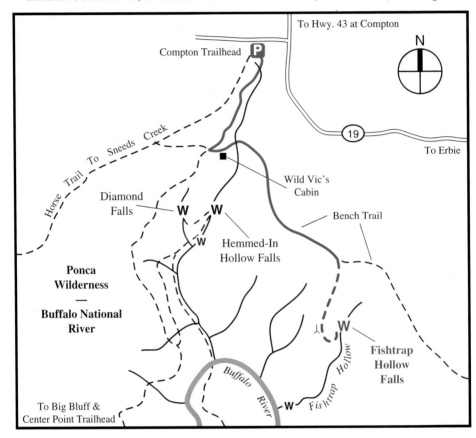

FISHTRAP HOLLOW FALLS. This is a tough waterfall to get in to and out of, but if you visit during high water, it's a real treat. The first part of the trek is on trails, but then you bushwhack down a really steep hillside, and it takes a great deal of *umph* to get back out. You could find the falls without it, but a GPS will make life a lot easier on you. *No dogs.*

The turnoff for the trailhead is located at Compton, between Harrison and Ponca on Hwy. 43. Take the gravel road across from the post office in Compton (CR#19), TURN RIGHT at the first intersection, and go just less than a mile and TURN RIGHT into the trailhead parking lot. There are two trails that leave this lot—the one on the right is a horse trail that goes down to Sneeds Creek.

Hike down the trail on the left, follow it across a small stream and then on down the rocky hillside. You will come to a trail intersection at .7—this is the Bench Trail and you TURN LEFT onto it. (The trail straight ahead goes down to Hemmed-In Hollow, and the trail to the right goes over to the horse trail to Sneeds Creek). You will pass Wild Vic's Cabin on the right after several hundred yards on the Bench Trail—worth a peek inside.

The Bench Trail is mostly used by horses, so you will have some muddy going. It follows along a mostly-level bench through what used to be an obvious homestead—look at the large stones that form rock walls along the trail. The trail drops on down the hill,

Fishtrap Hollow Falls (during high water)

crosses a couple of tiny drainages, and then somewhere around 1.5 you need to LEAVE THE ROAD TO THE RIGHT and begin to bushwhack down the hillside. There is no real landmark to help you find the spot—a GPS would help you find it easily.

The first part of the descent is gentle, but the slope turns steep in a hurry. There is a faint volunteer trail of sorts that goes down the middle of a small ridge, down to a sinkhole. You continue down past the sinkhole and through a small set of broken bluffs. TURN LEFT at the base of those and make your way down into Fishtrap Hollow. You want to find the top of the bluffs that form the narrow canyon. Once you do, TURN LEFT to get to the top of the falls. Or TURN RIGHT and find the downstream-end of the bluffs, make your way down through them, and follow the base of the bluffs back to the left and upstream to the bottom of the waterfall. It is *quite dangerous* all through here.

Emergency contact: Newton County Sheriff, 870–446–5124

Hideout Hollow Falls – ★★★★+ – 37′

2.0 miles roundtrip, easy hike, GPS not needed
Lat/Lon–36 04.848 N, 93 16.186 W • UTM–4 **75** 726 E, 39 **92** 735 N, Ponca Quad

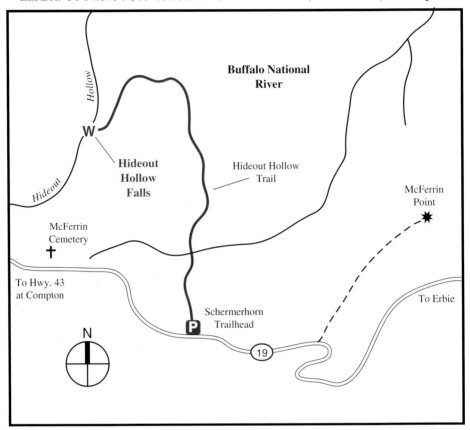

HIDEOUT HOLLOW FALLS. I'm not sure who used to hide out in this hollow (the re-mains of an old dwelling are under the bluff near the bottom of this waterfall), but they sure picked a great place to do it. There are numerous tall bluffs and giant slabs of stone in this area, plus the wonderful falls at the head of the canyon. The hike in is pretty easy, but if you have young folks with you hang on to them because the trail runs along the top of the bluffs and can be really dangerous (for adults too!). *No dogs allowed on the trail.*

The turnoff for the trailhead is located at Compton, between Harrison and Ponca on Hwy. 43. Take the gravel road across from the post office in Compton (CR#19), TURN RIGHT at the first intersection, go about 3.0 miles (past the Compton Trailhead for Hemmed-In Hollow), and TURN LEFT into the trailhead and PARK. This is called the Schermerhorn Trailhead after Jim Schermerhorn, who was an accomplished caver of world renown.

Follow the Hideout Hollow Trail down a little hill and across a stream, then up the other side and under a powerline. It levels out and comes to the edge of the bluffs that form the canyon wall, then curves around to the left. You'll have some nice views down into the canyon as the trail follows the top of the bluff all the way to the creek at the head of the canyon at 1.0. The falls is just downstream a few feet—the rocks are super slick there!

Emergency contact: Newton County Sheriff, 870–446–5124

Hideout Hollow Falls (during high water)

Hammerschmidt Falls – ★★★★+ – 43′

.4 mile roundtrip, easy bushwhack, GPS not needed

Lat/Lon–36 01.325 N, 93 17.282 W • UTM–4 **74** 062 E, 39 **86** 226 N, Ponca Quad

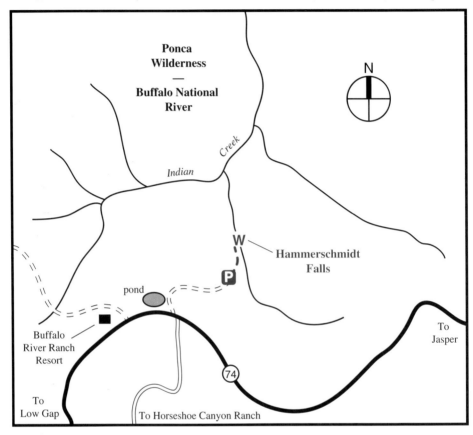

HAMMERSCHMIDT FALLS. This is the uppermost waterfall in what is perhaps the greatest of all canyons in the Ozarks. Indian Creek is filled with steep, rocky, sometimes nearly impassable terrain, caves, and lots of waterfalls. Most people will never see the rest of the waterfalls there, but this one is easy to get to and accessible to many folks. It is named after longtime Arkansas Congressman John Paul Hammerschmidt who helped get the legislation through Congress that created America's first National River.

The turnoff is located between Jasper and Low Gap on Hwy. 74. To get to the turnoff take Hwy. 74 east from Low Gap 2.4 miles (or 2.8 miles west of the turnoff to Kyles Landing) and TURN LEFT onto an unmarked jeep road. This turnoff is just across the highway from the turnoff to Horseshoe Canyon, which is marked. The first part of this road is good, but the last 100 yards are really bad and require a high clearance vehicle to negotiate. If you have a regular car, you will need to find a spot to pull off and park before you get to the end. Otherwise, simply take the road to a spot where it openes up on and PARK on the left, which is about .25 mile or so from the highway.

Hike down the old road trace a couple hundred feet to where a creek crosses the road—this is the creek that feeds the waterfall. TURN LEFT either before or after you cross the creek (depending on how wet your feet might get if you crossed it!) and follow the creek 100

John Paul Hammerschmidt Falls (foggy day during high water)

yards or so to the top of the falls. It is possible to make your way around and down to the base of the falls from either side of the creek. Like many waterfalls in the Ozarks, there is a redbud tree growing near the base that often comes alive with color in March.

I do not recommend following the creek all the way down the hillside through the canyon to the bottom unless you are an expert. You can come up to Copperhead Falls and Tunnel Cave Falls from the bottom (see directions on the next page).

Emergency contact: Newton County Sheriff, 870–446–5124

Copperhead Falls – ★★★★ – 13′

4.4 miles roundtrip, difficult bushwhack, GPS helpful
Lat/Lon–36 01.796 N, 93 17.259 W • UTM–4 **74** 099 E, 39 **87** 098 N, Ponca Quad

Tunnel Cave Falls – ★★★★★ – 31′

Same location as above, difficult bushwhack, GPS helpful
Lat/Lon–36 01.769 N, 93 17.254 W • UTM–4 **74** 107 E, 39 **87** 048 N, Ponca Quad

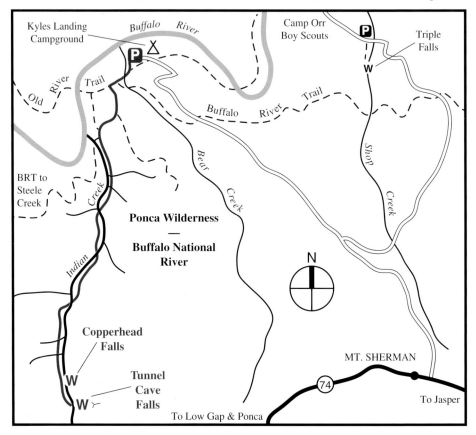

COPPERHEAD FALLS/TUNNEL CAVE FALLS. Most folks who make the trek up into Indian Creek talk about it for a long time afterward, and they seldom get back to the trailhead with any film left. One of the reasons that I consider this area to be perhaps the most scenic spot in Arkansas is because of these two waterfalls. And if you are there during or just after a really big rain, there will be waterfalls spilling off of nearly every bluff in the place, and it is quite amazing. The trip into the Indian Creek Canyon is a tough one though, and rather dangerous. The National Park Service says that more injuries happen in this canyon than at any other place in the park, so if you venture into it be *extremely* careful of what you are doing, take your time and watch your step, and don't blame me if you get hurt—I warned ya! *No dogs allowed on the trails.*

The turnoff to get to the parking area is located between Jasper and Low Gap. From Jasper, go west on Hwy. 74 to Mt. Sherman and TURN RIGHT at the sign for Kyles Landing (OR go east from Low Gap on Hwy. 74 for 5.2 miles to Mt. Sherman and TURN

Copperhead Falls
(A beautiful 2 x 3 foot color poster of this image is available for sale.)

LEFT at the Kyles Landing Sign). The road is gravel and normally not marked with a road number. Go 1.0 mile and TURN LEFT at the fork, then go 1.6 miles down a steep hill to the Kyles Landing Campground. TURN LEFT after the bathhouse and go all the way back to the trailhead and PARK. This is one of the major canoe access points for the river, and can get rather crowded on spring weekends. There is access for the Buffalo River Trail (BRT) and the Old River Trail (ORT—primarily used by horses) too, so you will need to follow the hiking directions carefully.

From the trailhead take off behind the bulletin board where you will immediately intersect with the ORT that comes in from the left—STAY STRAIGHT here and go across Bear Creek a few feet ahead. Just after you cross that creek, the BRT to Erbie takes off to the left—keep going STRAIGHT AHEAD on an old road bed. Just 100 yards after that intersection you will want to TURN LEFT onto the BRT going towards Steele Creek and leave the road bed and head uphill on another road bed. There are posts at most intersections that will help explain things. This roadbed climbs up a little bit then levels out, and you will pass a primitive trail that goes off to the left—keep going STRAIGHT AHEAD on the BRT. The trail drops down the hill to yet another intersection—TURN LEFT there. Soon after there is another intersection at .5—GO STRAIGHT. (The BRT turns to the right and crosses the normally-dry Indian Creek at this point, on its way to Steele Creek.) You are now heading up into the Indian Creek drainage and off of the BRT. The National Park Service does not recognize the trail from this point on as an official trail, and it is not marked or maintained in any way. But the area gets so much traffic that there is a pretty well-defined trail much of the way ahead, and we are going to follow it.

(By the way, as a side note about accuracy, we had a heck of a time trying to figure out if "Steele" Creek had an "e" on the end of it or not. Most references in books and on maps, even the USGS topos, show it as "Steel." But I found an obscure reference to the original pioneer who settled the area, and his name was indeed "Steele." It just so happened that my friend Bob Chester worked with this guy's grandson, and sure enough, the name has been printed incorrectly in books and on maps for many years—it should be Steele Creek.)

The "trail" follows alongside Indian Creek upstream and it is a gentle grade for the next half mile. Then the trail crosses Indian Creek for the first of three times. On the other side the trail heads up the hill a little, then levels out and continues going upstream. There will be numerous trails from this point on, some up on the hillside, others down along the creek. Choose the route that seems best to you, but do keep in mind that the rocks down next to the creek are *extremely* slick!

The trail will cross the creek a second time, climb up onto the opposite bank and head still further up into the drainage. Just after the third crossing of the creek, take the trail that heads *steeply* up the hillside and away from the creek. The hillside is getting eroded pretty badly, and this is one example why the Park Service should construct an actual trail through here because the traffic is damaging the resource.

It is a tough climb, but short, and soon the trail levels out and then runs along on top of a bluff. The path is narrow and treacherous through here—one slip and they will have to call out for a body bag! But the view is incredible from up there. Eventually the trail makes its way back down to the creek, and follows along beside it. Soon you will come to Copperhead Falls at 2.2, which is on the creek next to the trail down on your LEFT. Be careful of those slick rock layers!

This waterfall got its name from me, and it was the very first waterfall that I ever named. While I was standing there one frigid March morning taking the photo that is shown on the previous page there was a copperhead snake coiled up right next to my camera bag the entire time. He seemed to enjoy watching me work, and I didn't mind the company. The color version of that photo appears on page 83 in my *Arkansas Wilderness* picture book, and I will be happy to sell you a copy of the big poster of it!

Continue up the creek past the falls and you will enter the main Indian Creek Canyon, and come to Tunnel Cave Falls after only another few hundred feet. This immediate area is one of the most spectacular spots in all of Arkansas. The creek actually enters Tunnel Cave upstream a ways, runs through the cave and pours out of the mouth of the cave right down into the middle of this canyon. The walls are lined with ferns, and it is one amazing sight. Folks also call this Arkansas Cave, but I prefer Neil Compton's name for it, Tunnel Falls. The photo at right is on page 35 in my *Arkansas Wilderness* picture book.

Tunnel Cave Falls (aka Arkansas Cave Falls)

Until recently the cave was the main route to go upstream for hikers, but it has now been closed off to entry all year long to protect bat populations—*do not enter the cave!* The canyon is blocked by a wall of rock right after the cave (and often a waterfall tumbles down that wall). There is a way to continue on up the canyon, but it involves climbing up ledges, scrambling up steep slopes, inching along a narrow ledge where one slip would result in serious injury, and crawling through a tunnel. The famous Eye of the Needle is upstream less than .25 mile, and other great sights, but the risk is too great and I do not recommend further travel to anyone but the most experienced and those willing to risk it all. It is best to savor this incredible area, then turn around and return to the trailhead.

Emergency contact: Newton County Sheriff, 870–446–5124

Triple Falls – ★★★★★ – 48′

.5 mile roundtrip, easy hike, GPS not needed

Lat/Lon–36 03.282 N, 93 15.498 W • UTM–4 **76** 751 E, 39 **89** 837 N, Ponca Quad

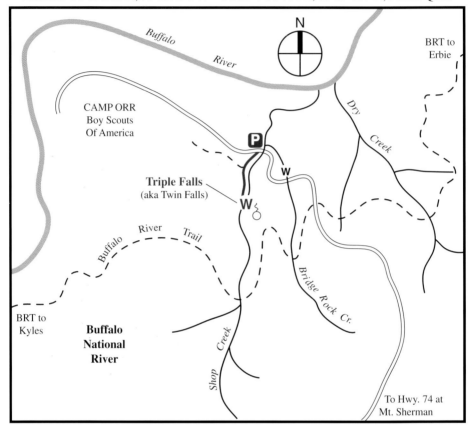

TRIPLE FALLS (aka Twin Falls) at Camp Orr. This is one of the most scenic easy water-falls to get to—even kids can walk right up to the edge of the creek near the base for a perfect view. It has long been called Twin Falls, but I call it Triple Falls for two reasons: first, when the falls are running well there are always three falls, not two, and I have grown tired of everyone asking me how come it is called Twin Falls if there are actually three falls! And secondly we have so many other waterfalls named Twin Falls in Arkansas it is simply less confusing to call this one something else. The name "twin" comes from the fact (I think) that there are actually two water sources that feed the falls from above—one is the creek (the right falls), and the other is a spring up to the left that feeds the two falls on the left. So now you know. *No dogs allowed on the trail.*

The turnoff to get to the parking area is located between Jasper and Low Gap. From Jasper, go west on Hwy. 74 to Mt. Sherman and TURN RIGHT at the sign for Kyles Landing (OR go east from Low Gap on Hwy. 74 for 5.2 miles to Mt. Sherman and TURN LEFT at the Kyles Landing Sign) The road is gravel and normally not marked with a road number. Go 1.0 mile and BEAR RIGHT at the fork—the left fork goes down into Kyles Landing. Continue heading down the hill for another 1.8 miles until you hit bottom right after crossing a creek and PARK at the edge of a field (there may be a sign for Twin Falls there). NOTE that the last mile of this road is *really steep* and muddy!

Triple Falls (aka Twin Falls)

From the parking area head to the left on a trail that follows that creek you just crossed upstream into the woods—it's a level hike of less than .25 mile. There will be another trail that comes in from your right, but just keep going STRAIGHT AHEAD and you will come right to the falls.

NOTE that the land beyond the parking area is the Boy Scout facility Camp Orr, and generally off limits to the public. Scouts from all over the region come there to learn outdoor skills each summer—I was one of them when I was a "tenderfoot" scout in the 1960's. One of the things I remember most about my trip was hearing about the Legend of Smokey Joe. This is a tale that I believe was created to help explain the existence of the Buffalo Bigfoot, a creature that has been reported up and down the Buffalo drainage for many generations, going all the way back to the mid 1800's, and perhaps even before. Is it possible he is still out there today?

Emergency contact: Newton County Sheriff, 870–446–5124

Thunder Canyon Falls – ★★★★★ – 71′

4.0 miles roundtrip, medium hike/bushwhack, GPS recommended

Lat/Lon–36 05.076 N, 93 15.257 W • UTM–4 **77** 122 E, 39 **93** 152 N, Ponca Quad

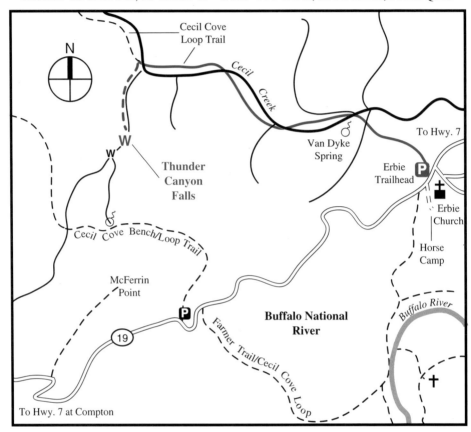

THUNDER CANYON FALLS. When I first approached this falls I could hear a distant roar, or the sound of thunder, coming from the waterfall. When I rounded the corner and stepped into this incredible little canyon I was stunned at the sight of the falls. I consider it one of the most scenic waterfalls in Arkansas, and few people have ever seen it. *No dogs.*

The turnoff for the trailhead is located at Compton, between Harrison and Ponca on Hwy. 43. Take the gravel road across from the post office in Compton (CR#19), TURN RIGHT at the first intersection, go about 6 miles (past the Compton and Hideout Hollow trailheads), down a steep, winding and *very* rough road to the Erbie Trailhead on the left and PARK. (You may need a 4wd vehicle to get through one long stretch of soft clay on this road, especially during the wet season.) You can also get to the trailhead by following FR#19 from near Dogpatch on Hwy. 7, or from Hwy. 7 via CR#80 & CR#57 (turn just north of the Pruitt bridge and stay left until you get to Erbie). You can also get here by crossing the river at Erbie, but during good waterfall flow periods the river will probably be much too high to ford.

From the trailhead the trail heads on down the hill to Cecil Creek where it crosses just below Van Dyke Spring. Continue on the trail as it follows Cecil Creek upstream on the level, crossing the creek several times. This is a nice, easy stroll through the valley. Just after you cross the creek for a fourth time at 1.4, LEAVE THE TRAIL and hike BACK TO

Thunder Canyon Falls (during high water)

THE LEFT and over to a stream that flows into Cecil Creek. TURN RIGHT and follow this creek upstream. There are many places where the creekbed is solid rock carved out by the rushing waters, and you will have to climb up onto and hike across the steep hillside above—pick your way the best you can. After about a half mile of this at 2.0 you will enter Thunder Canyon and will hear the falls. The waterfall is at the end of the short box canyon. You cannot actually see the top of the falls—it continues on up and out of sight. (We had to rappel down from above to measure this one.) The falls have drilled a hole in the bottom of the canyon about 20 feet in diameter and 14 feet deep. The canyon wall on one side arches completely over your head. It is a remarkable spot.

Emergency contact: Newton County Sheriff, 870–446–5124

Broadwater Hollow – ★★★★ – 21′

.6 mile roundtrip, easy bushwhack, GPS not needed

Lat/Lon–36 06.300 N, 93 16.024 W • UTM–4 **75** 977 E, 39 **95** 418 N, Ponca Quad

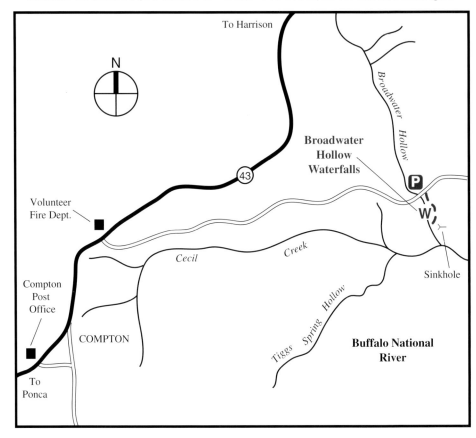

BROADWATER HOLLOW. There isn't one specific waterfall in this hollow that makes it special, but rather a number of them, all connected by the tumbling waters of Broadwater Hollow. You can drive right to the upper end of it, making access easy.

From the Compton post office go north on Hwy. 43 for .8 miles and TURN RIGHT onto a gravel road (the turn is right across from the Volunteer Fire Station). Follow this road 2.0 miles until you come to the crossing of Broadwater Hollow—PARK on the hill just before you get to the creek, or you can cross the creek and park right there. The property upstream from the parking area is private, so stay below the road while hiking.

There is a trail of sorts on the east side of the creek that heads down the hill alongside the stream—follow this trail and you will see several waterfalls, cascades and pouroffs on your right. One of them is pictured on pages 6–7 in my ***Buffalo River Wilderness*** picture book. It was shot from behind the waterfall looking out. The waterfall pictured here is the next falls down from that one.

If you follow the trail down far enough you will come to a sink hole on your left. This creek eventually feeds into Cecil Creek and flows past Thunder Canyon, home to another terrific waterfall in this Buffalo River country.

Emergency contact: Newton County Sheriff, 870–446–5124

Broadwater Hollow

Liles Falls – ★★★★ – 41′

.2 mile roundtrip, easy bushwhack, GPS not needed

Lat/Lon–36 03.428 N, 93 11.729 W • UTM–4 **82** 409 E, 39 **90** 094 N, Jasper Quad

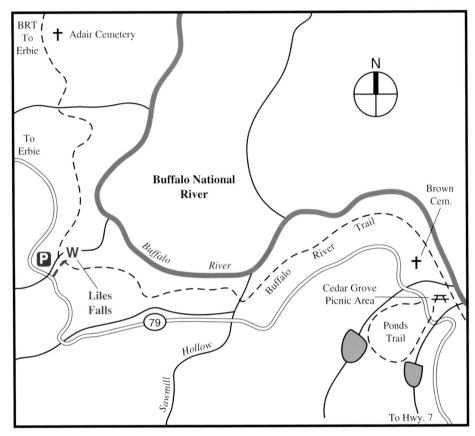

LILES FALLS. This waterfall is really beautiful when the water is high, and it is so simple to get to! The falls is named after Jim Liles, former Assistant Superintendent with Buffalo National River. He was in charge of developing the trail systems in the early days of the Park, and had a great deal to do with their design, layout and construction (he even spent a lot of time building trails himself, on his days off). We have a great trail system at the Park thanks to Jim!

The turnoff is located between Jasper and Pruitt on Hwy. 7. TURN WEST onto CR#79 (gravel)—it is marked as the turnoff to Erbie Campground. Go 3.5 miles (1.5 miles past the Cedar Grove Picnic Area—there is a short, easy loop trail there that is great for kids), and PARK just after you cross the small creek that runs across the road. This creek is the one that feeds the waterfall, so it should be running well.

To get to the falls, go back and cross the creek next to the parking area, and then head downhill into the woods. There is no trail and you simply follow the creek for a couple hundred yards—you will come to and cross the Buffalo River Trail near the top of the falls. The creek runs into the Buffalo River a little ways below the falls.

Emergency contact: Newton County Sheriff, 870–446–5124

Jim Liles Falls

Hudson Shelter Falls – ★★★★ – 24′

.8 miles roundtrip, easy bushwhack, GPS helpful

Lat/Lon–35 51.089 N, 93 07.447 W • UTM–4 **88** 808 E, 39 **67** 274 N, Lurton Quad

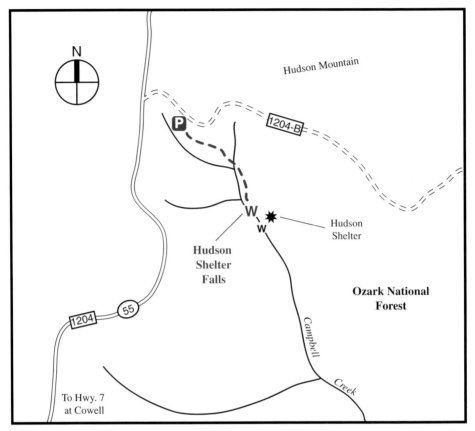

HUDSON SHELTER FALLS. When I first went to this falls it was nearly dark and I just barely had time to snap a photo and hike back out to the truck. When I returned later to measure the height of the waterfall I found there was a second falls just below the upper one, and it too was over 20 feet tall. These falls are named for the bluff shelter that they pour over, which is one of the deepest shelters in the Ozarks—it goes back under the bluff more than 75 feet, and provides a nice level spot for a picnic lunch. (*Please note* that there is no digging or collecting of artifacts allowed in our national forests!) While there is no trail down to this waterfall, it is a short, easy bushwhack to get down to it.

To get to the parking area go south from Jasper on Hwy. 7 about 14 miles to the intersection with Hwy. 16. Continue south on Hwy. 7/16 another 2.9 miles to Cowell and TURN LEFT onto FR#1204/CR#55 (gravel). Go 4.2 miles and TURN RIGHT onto FR#1204-B. Go just a 100 yards or so and pull over and PARK ON THE RIGHT where an old log road takes off to the right.

Head down the old log road for about 100 yards and when it begins to swing back to the left, LEAVE the road trace to the LEFT and begin to bushwhack straight down the hillside. There is a small creek on the right and one on the left that will come together down in front of you—keep following the water downhill and you will get to the upper

Upper Hudson Shelter Falls

falls in another couple hundred yards. As always, be very careful if you decide to get down to the lower falls and the shelter below.

Emergency contact: Newton County Sheriff, 870–446–5124

Dogwood Falls – ★★★★ – 37′

1.2 miles roundtrip, medium bushwhack, GPS recommended
Lat/Lon–35 50.987 N, 92 59.073 W • UTM–5 **01** 409 E, 39 **67** 078 N, Moore Quad

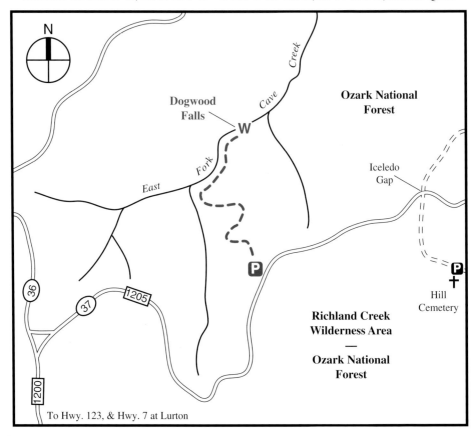

DOGWOOD FALLS. There are many dogwood trees growing at the base of waterfalls in the Ozarks, but for some reason this one is especially pleasing. I'm not sure if dogwood trees enjoy looking at waterfalls, or they simply want a constant drink!

Take Hwy. 123 (paved) east out of Lurton (located on Hwy. 7 north of Pelsor and south of Cowell). Go 1.5 miles and TURN RIGHT onto FR#1200/CR#36 (gravel). Go 6.8 miles and TURN RIGHT onto FR#1205/CR#37. Go 1.1 and PARK on the left side of the road, under a powerline. If coming from the other direction, take FR#1205 north from Richland Creek Campground and go .4 mile past Iceledo Gap and PARK on the right.

Head off into the woods to your left, under the powerline, and then DOWN the hill. There is no trail, just a steep hill between you and the waterfall. Once you get to the creek at the bottom of this hill TURN RIGHT and follow the creek downhill. That will lead you to the top of Dogwood Falls at .6.

Emergency contact: Newton County Sheriff, 870–446–5124

Dogwood Falls

Hamilton Falls – ★★★★ – 12′

4.6 miles roundtrip, medium-difficult bushwhack, GPS recommended

Lat/Lon–35 48.713 N, 92 57.838 W • UTM–5 **03** 271 E, 39 **62** 876 N, Moore Quad

Twin Falls of Richland – ★★★★★ –17′/19′

Add 1.0 (5.6 roundtrip total), difficult bushwhack, GPS recommended

Lat/Lon–35 48.349 N, 92 57.844 W • UTM–5 **03** 261 E, 39 **62** 202 N, Moore Quad

Richland Falls – ★★★★+ – 8′

Add 1.0 (6.6 roundtrip total), difficult bushwhack, GPS recommended

Lat/Lon–35 48.051 N, 92 57.609 W • UTM–5 **03** 616 E, 39 **61** 652 N, Moore Quad

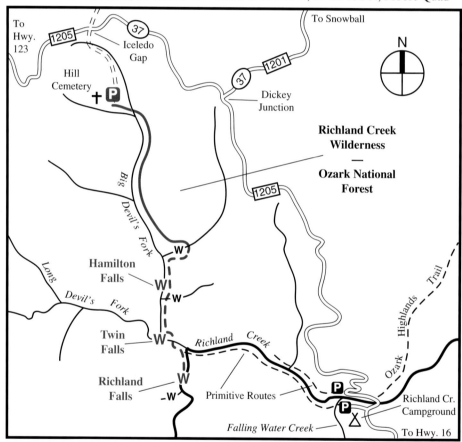

HAMILTON FALLS/TWIN FALLS/RICHLAND FALLS. The Richland Creek Wilderness area is rich with waterfalls and tumbling cascades—you will find them in nearly every drainage no matter how small. Twin Falls of Richland (aka Twin Falls of Devil's Fork) is one of the most classic of all Ozark waterfalls, and one of the most photographed. There are several different ways to get into it—including going up Richland Creek from the campground, which is quite scenic; and taking the primitive trail on the north side of the campground and creek (this unofficial trail disappears part way up and turns into a scramble across a steep hillside). Someday we hope to have an official maintained trail

72

Twin Falls of Richland

into Twin Falls, but for now my favorite route is to come down from Hill Cemetery, passing several other waterfalls on the way down. Much of this route is along an old road and the hiking is easy, but the rest of the way can be some pretty tough bushwhacking, so it is rated difficult.

Take Hwy. 123 (paved) east out of Lurton (located on Hwy. 7 north of Pelsor and south of Cowell). Go 1.5 miles and TURN RIGHT onto FR#1200/CR#36 (gravel). Go 6.8 miles and TURN RIGHT onto FR#1205/CR#37. Go 1.6 miles and TURN RIGHT at the bottom of the hill—this is Iceledo Gap. Take this little road down the hill past a house and across a stream. It will end after .8 at Hill Cemetery. (Road is getting bad-may need 4wd.)

Hike down the hill to the left of the cemetery on an old road trace that has been closed. It will cross Big Devil's Fork right away, then swing to the right and follow the creek downstream (the road is out in the woods and you don't see the creek). Stay on this old road until you get to a creek crossing and nice waterfall just below the road to the right at 1.8. Now you have a couple of options. If you have a GPS or a good map you can continue on the road another .5 mile and then bushwhack down to Twin Falls, OR go the way that I do, which is much more scenic, but a lot tougher on the feet and body.

From the waterfall next to the road follow the road on around the curve to the right, then LEAVE THE ROAD TO THE RIGHT and go down to the stream below the falls. Follow this creek downstream where it soon hits Big Devil's Fork (some interesting cascades along the way). TURN LEFT and follow Big Devil's Fork downstream. (You can also simply follow along up above the creek, looking down on it, until you can see or hear the next waterfall.)

At 2.3 you will come to Hamilton Falls, a beautiful little waterfall that empties into an emerald pool (photo on next page). Don Hamilton was one of the leaders of the Arkansas Wilderness Coalition in the early 1980's when we were fighting to establish wilderness

Don Hamilton Falls

areas. His influence and expertise helped us secure protection for many wilderness areas in Arkansas, including Richland Creek. He is one of the most eloquent public speakers that I have ever heard.

When the water is up and running well, there is another waterfall just downstream from Hamilton Falls that pours over the east side of the canyon. There are some giant boulders at the base of the falls to welcome the water to Big Devil's Fork.

CONTINUE downstream from there another .5 until you come to Twin Falls at 2.8. NOTE that the area around the falls is quite fragile and easily messed up and trashed out. If you choose to camp in this area, do so elsewhere and *not* near the waterfall. Thanks! There are waterfalls up Long Devil's Fork too that are worth exploring.

To get to Richland Falls, you need to cross the creek below Twin Falls. There is a volunteer trail on the other side—TURN LEFT and follow that trail downstream to where Devil's Fork meets Richland Creek. TURN RIGHT and continue to follow the trail as it heads upstream on Richland. Just keep on going and you will come to Richland Falls before too long at 3.3. This falls is not too tall, but it spans the entire creek. It is tough to get a good photo of this falls because it is so wide. I like to isolate one section of it with a long lens instead of trying to get the entire thing in the picture.

If you are at Richland Falls when the water is low there will be many different waterfalls instead of just one wide one. When the weather is warm each of the individual falls can have a different water temperature, depending on how deep the pool is upstream that is feeding it. The sun will heat the shallow pools more than the deep ones. Also, there are some terrific exposed fossil beds to look for in low water upstream.

Richland Falls

There is a good place to camp up on the bench to the west of Richland Falls (to the right as you are looking upstream). An old road goes up to the camp area from the base of the falls. The first time I camped there the temperature got down to 17 degrees below zero! We had hiked in from Richland Campground, and so had to cross the creek twice in that frigid weather in order to get back to our car. It also had snowed about a foot that night and I got some great winter pictures on the way out.

Emergency contact: Newton County Sheriff, 870-446-5124

Falling Water Falls – ★★★★ – 10′

View from car, GPS not needed

Lat/Lon–35 43.317 N, 92 56.964 W • UTM–5 **04** 592 E, 39 **52** 902 N, Smyrna Quad

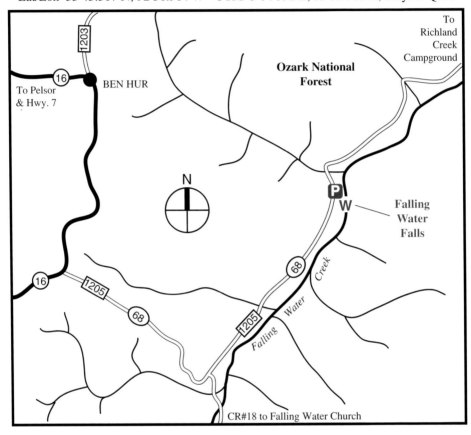

FALLING WATER FALLS. Here is a scenic waterfall right next to the road that is also a terrific swimming hole. I've even seen a baptism take place there. And to see what else goes on there see page 104 in my *Arkansas Spring* picture book.

To get to the falls, take Hwy. 16 east from Pelsor (on Hwy. 7 between Russellville and Jasper). Go about nine miles to Ben Hur (past the parking area for Kings Bluff Falls), then continue past Ben Hur about a mile and TURN LEFT onto FR#1205/CR#68 (gravel). Go 2.3 miles and PARK along the road, next to the waterfall which is down on the right. To get to Falling Water Falls from Richland Creek Campground, head south on FR#1205 and follow it for about 7 miles and the falls will be on the left.

You may also want to visit the other waterfalls that are downstream—see the next couple of pages for photos and descriptions.

Emergency contact: Pope County Sheriff, 479–967–9300.

Falling Water Falls (note road in background)

Falling Water Falls (during high water)

Six Finger Falls – ★★★ – 6'

100 feet from road, GPS helpful

Lat/Lon–35 45.716 N, 92 56.252 W • UTM–5 **05** 662 E, 39 **57** 336 N, Moore Quad

Fuzzybutt Falls – ★★★★ – 16'

.2 mile roundtrip, easy bushwhack, GPS helpful

Lat/Lon–35 45.821 N, 92 56.303 W • UTM–5 **05** 585 E, 39 **57** 531 N, Moore Quad

Keefe Falls – ★★★★+ – 78'

1.0 mile roundtrip, easy/medium bushwhack, GPS helpful

Lat/Lon–35 45.929 N, 92 55.565 W • UTM–5 **06** 697 E, 39 **57** 730 N, Moore Quad

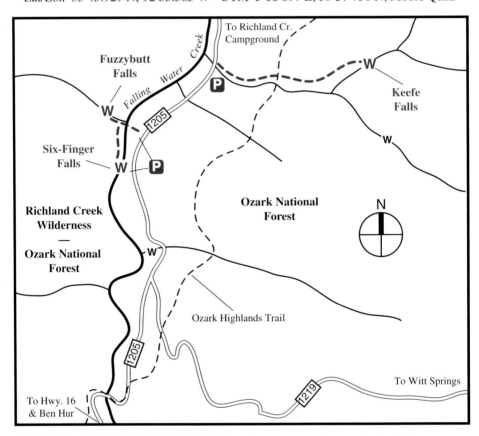

SIX FINGER/FUZZYBUTT/KEEFE FALLS. You can get to three entirely different water-falls along a short stretch of road next to Falling Water Creek. This river runs along the edge of the Richland Creek Wilderness area, which contains many great waterfalls and other scenic areas. Further exploration on your part may reveal lots of neat stuff.

To get to the first falls, take Hwy. 16 east from Pelsor (on Hwy. 7 between Rus-sellville and Jasper). Go about nine miles to Ben Hur (past the parking area for Kings Bluff Falls), then continue past Ben Hur about a mile and TURN LEFT onto FR#1205/CR#68 (gravel). Follow this road past Falling Water Falls for 5.7 miles to the intersection with FR#1219 (this will be about .4 after you cross over Falling Water Creek on a bridge).

Six Finger Falls (the rest of the fingers are out of view)

Go about .3 and PARK in a little pulloff on the LEFT side of the road. Falling Water Creek and Six Finger Falls will be right in front of you through the trees.

To get to Fuzzybutt Falls (photo on next page) you can either hike downstream a couple of hundred yards from Six Finger Falls, or drive down the road to the next pulloff on the left and PARK. You will have to wade across Falling Water Creek—remember *do not cross any water that is running high and too muddy for you to see the bottom!* Cross the creek and find the entrance to the canyon just on the other side—there will be a stream coming out of it and running into the creek. This is a narrow canyon cut into layers of shale rock. The canyon is only a couple hundred feet long and ends at Fuzzybutt Falls. You can probably guess how this waterfall got its name (it was really cold that day, and it was painful to take this picture!). My wife asked me include the photo, but the forest service labeled it as "obscene" and had banned the original black & white book from their sales outlets—I "fuzzed" up my better side a bit for this new color edition.

Keefe Falls is going to take a bit more work to get to (turn page for photo). Drive down the road another quarter mile (.6 from the previous intersection with FR#1219) to where a creek comes from the right and goes under the road—PARK where you can. You can also get to this spot from Richland Creek Campground—go south on FR#1205 for 2.8 miles and PARK at the stream crossing.

There is no trail so it is all bushwhacking, but it will be easy to find the falls—simply hike into the woods and follow the little creek upstream as best you can. You will come to and cross the Ozark Highlands Trail right away. This is at the 141 mile point on the trail. Continue up the creek. I like to veer off up to the left and climb up to the base of a very tall bluff up there, then follow this bluff to the right all the way to Keefe Falls. The lower areas of this bluff are made up of many layers of shale rock, but the upper layers are more traditional solid layers. If you stay down on the creek, STAY LEFT when you come to a fork. You will find Keefe Falls at the head of the hollow at .5.

Fuzzybutt Falls

Terry Keefe Falls

Keefe Falls is named after one of the great waterfall hunters in the Ozarks, Terry Keefe. He has taken me to countless unknown waterfalls and other scenic places over the years, and has always done so at a pretty good clip I might add. I can keep up a fast pace myself, but he has run off and left me on numerous occasions.

Emergency contact: Searcy County Sheriff, 870–448–2340

Stack Rock Homestead Falls – ★★★★ – 35′

2.0 miles roundtrip, easy hike, GPS helpful

Lat/Lon–35 52.471 N, 92 55.823 W • UTM–5 **06** 300 E, 39 **69** 824 N, Moore Quad

Dry Creek Falls – ★★★★ – 20′

Add 3.4 to above (5.4 total), difficult bushwhack, GPS recommended

Lat/Lon–35 52.547 N, 92 56.434 W • UTM–5 **05** 381 E, 39 **69** 964 N, Eula Quad

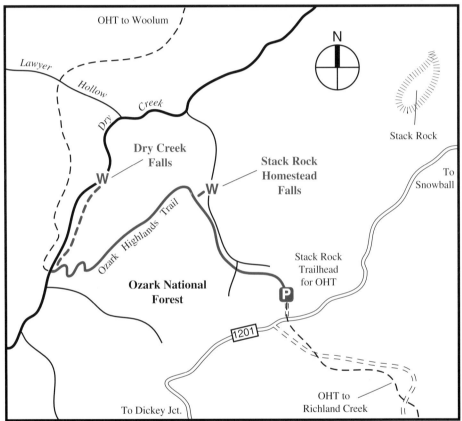

STACK ROCK HOMESTEAD/DRY CREEK FALLS. Both of these falls are accessible from the Ozark Highlands Trail (OHT)—one is right on the trail and the other via a bushwhack. They are in quite scenic locations and well worth the effort to get to.

Take Hwy. 123 (paved) east out of Lurton (located on Hwy. 7 north of Pelsor and south of Cowell). Go 1.5 miles and TURN RIGHT onto FR#1200/CR#36 (gravel). Go 6.8 miles and TURN RIGHT onto FR#1205/CR#37. Go 3.4 miles to Dickey Junction and TURN LEFT onto FR#1201. Go 3.0 miles and TURN LEFT into the trailhead and PARK.

The trail heads out of the parking area to the north on an old jeep road, then soon leaves the road TO THE LEFT. It drops on down the hill, past OHT milepost #152, across a creek, and then levels out at 1.0 where there used to be a pioneer homesite. The stone chimney is off the trail to the left. Stack Rock Homestead Falls is just below the trail TO THE RIGHT—go down to the creek and follow it to the top of the falls.

To get to Dry Creek Falls, CONTINUE hiking along the OHT. It will run level for a while, past OHT milepost #153, then begin to switchback down the hillside, coming to

Stack Rock Homestead Falls (above), **Dry Creek Falls** (below)

Dry Creek at 2.0. (Contrary to the name, there is almost always water in Dry Creek!)

This is where the fun stuff begins. TURN RIGHT at the creek and follow it downstream, bushwhacking however you can. If the water is high you should not cross the creek. Continue down the creek—past several neat water features, including a couple of long whitewater slides—and you will come to Dry Creek Falls at 2.7.

Emergency contact: Searcy County Sheriff, 870–448–2340

Vickor Falls – ★★★★ – 43'

1.8 miles roundtrip, easy hike/bushwhack, GPS helpful

Lat/Lon–36 01.114 N, 92 25.881 W • UTM–5 51 254 E, 39 85 949 N, Big Flat Quad

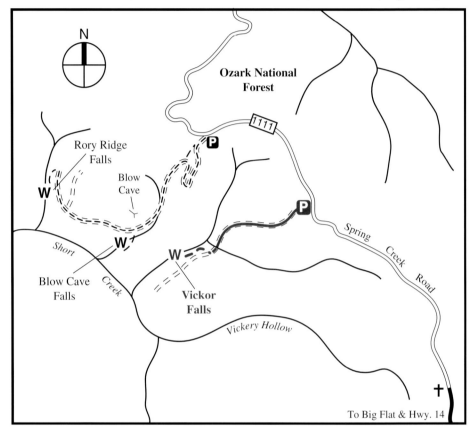

VICKOR FALLS. This is the first of several nice waterfalls that you can get to along this road. And it's a pretty easy hike to get to each one. These waterfalls look especially good when the water is high. NOTE: When the water is high this road may not be passable farther up north where the road runs through Spring Creek.

From Big Flat on Hwy. 14, head out Spring Creek Road/FR#1111. It starts out as pavement (CR#135), but soon changes to gravel at the cemetery—zero the odometer there. Go 1.5 miles and PARK where a jeep road takes off down the hill to the left. If you have a 4wd vehicle you might be able to drive most of the way to the falls, but we'll begin the counter from the main gravel road.

Hike along the jeep road as it drops on down the hill, bearing to the LEFT when it comes into an open area near the bottom. Just after that it crosses a creek at .7. You have two options here: to get to the top of the falls TURN RIGHT just after crossing this creek and follow a faint trail downstream several hundred yards to the top of the falls at .9. OR, to get down to the bottom of the falls CONTINUE on the jeep road, uphill and to the right just a little bit. It will soon level off. After .5 mile or so LEAVE THE ROAD and bushwhack down to the right and find a way down through the bluff. Then follow the base of the bluff or the creek to THE RIGHT until you come to the base of the falls.

Vickor Falls

If you have a GPS and are good at cross-country travel, you might want to bushwhack from the top of this falls on over to Blow Cave Falls, which is in the next hollow over. From there you could easily get to Rory Ridge Falls too. OR you could follow this creek downstream to Short Creek, turn right and go downstream until you got to the next creek, then follow it upstream to Blow Cave Falls. Lots of possibilities if you are comfortable in the woods. The rest of us will hike back out to the car and take a different route in!

Emergency contact: Searcy County Sheriff, 870–448–2340

Blow Cave Falls – ★★★★ – 40′

1.4 miles roundtrip, easy hike/bushwhack, GPS helpful

Lat/Lon–36 01.190 N, 92 26.169 W • UTM–5 **50** 822 E, 39 **86** 087 N, Big Flat Quad

Rory Ridge Falls – ★★★★★ – 52′

Add 1.4 to above, easy hike/bushwhack, GPS helpful

Lat/Lon–36 01.451 N, 92 26.623 W • UTM–5 **50** 137 E, 39 **86** 565 N, Big Flat Quad

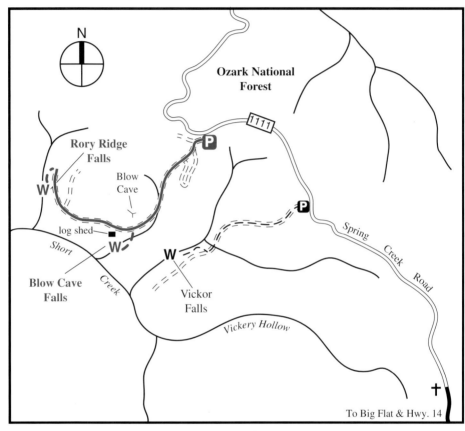

BLOW CAVE FALLS/RORY RIDGE FALLS. Visit these falls when there is high water.

From Big Flat on Hwy. 14, head out Spring Creek Road/FR#1111. It starts out as pavement (CR#135), but soon changes to gravel at the cemetery—zero your odometer there. Go 2.4 miles and PARK on the left. If you have a 4wd vehicle you might be able to drive most of the way to the falls, but we'll begin the counter from the main gravel road.

From the parking area head out on the jeep road, bearing to the LEFT at a fork just ahead. Then as the road curves around to the left, take the RIGHT fork that heads down a steep hill. Follow this road through the little valley and around to the right where it will come to a spring coming out of Blow Cave just up to your right at .7. To get to Blow Cave Falls, TURN LEFT and follow the spring water downstream a short distance to the falls. To get to Rory Ridge Falls, CONTINUE on the jeep road another .7, take the LEFT FORK and remain level, then TURN LEFT when you come to an old home foundation and bushwhack down the hill to the top of the falls just below (easy hike to the base of it).

Emergency contact: Searcy County Sheriff, 870–448–2340

Blow Cave Falls

Rory Ridge Falls

Cougar Falls – ★★★★★ – 77'

.6 mile roundtrip, easy bushwhack, GPS helpful
Lat/Lon–36 02.433 N, 92 22.611 W • UTM–5 **56** 150 E, 39 **88** 417 N, Big Flat Quad

China Falls – ★★★★+ – 68'

.5 mile roundtrip, easy bushwhack, GPS recommended
Lat/Lon–36 02.628 N, 92 23.018 W • UTM–5 **55** 536 E, 39 **88** 773 N, Big Flat Quad

Little Glory Hole – ★★★+ – 18'

.6 mile roundtrip, easy bushwhack, GPS recommended
Lat/Lon–36 02.905 N, 92 23.162 W • UTM–5 **55** 317 E, 39 **89** 284 N, Big Flat Quad

Crosscut Falls – ★★★★+ – 53'

.6 mile roundtrip, easy bushwhack, GPS recommended
Lat/Lon–36 03.029 N, 92 23.523 W • UTM–5 **54** 773 E, 39 **89** 509 N, Big Flat Quad

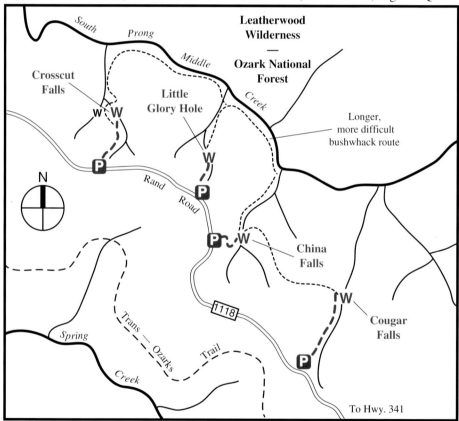

COUGAR/CHINA/LITTLE GLORY HOLE/CROSSCUT FALLS. Here are four beautiful waterfalls all in a line just inside the Leatherwood Wilderness. It is possible to do one longer and more difficult bushwhack loop from Cougar Falls to visit all of them and come in from the bottom of each (4.5 miles roundtrip—bushwhack 3.2, plus 1.3 along road), but we are going to take the easiest route to each one, requiring short drives along the road. Save these for the monsoon season—they look best with a *lot* of water.

Cougar Falls

From Big Flat, go 3.8 miles east on Hwy. 14 and TURN LEFT onto Hwy. 341 (paved). Go 2.3 miles and TURN LEFT onto Rand Road/FR#1118 (gravel). Go 1.2 miles and PARK on the RIGHT where you can for Cougar Falls. PARK at 1.9 for China, 2.1 for Little Glory Hole, and 2.5 for Crosscut. It will be easy to find all of this with a GPS.

To get to **Cougar Falls**, simply head down the hill from the road into the drainage and follow the little creek. You will come to the top of Cougar Falls at .3. There is a spot on the left that you can drop down to in order to get the same view as pictured above.

China Falls

To get to **China Falls**, drive on the road another .7 and PARK. Bushwhack down the hill to your right—it gets steep, so take it easy and zig-zag on the way back up. If you hit the bluffline going in, TURN RIGHT to get to the falls, if you hit the creek, TURN LEFT and follow it to the top of the falls. This falls was named after a favorite horse that Helen Elsner was riding when she first found these falls.

To get to **Little Glory Hole,** drive on the road another .2 and PARK. Drop down into the drainage and follow the creek down to the falls. This one isn't too tall but is interesting because the creek has drilled a hole into the roof of the bluff, creating a miniature waterfall in the same vein as the famous Glory Hole, described elsewhere in this book.

To get to **Crosscut Falls,** drive on the road another .4 and PARK. Work your way down into the drainage and follow the creek downstream to the top of the falls. There is another neat falls off on the left, and also a place where you can get down below the bluff. This falls gets its name from an old crosscut saw that was found nearby.

Emergency contact: Baxter County Sheriff, 870–425–6222

Little Glory Hole

Crosscut Falls

Funnel Falls (2) – ★★★★★ – 41'/52'

1.0 mile roundtrip, medium bushwhack, GPS helpful

Lat/Lon–36 04.185 N, 92 26.304 W • UTM–5 **50** 587 E, 39 **91** 622 N, Big Flat Quad

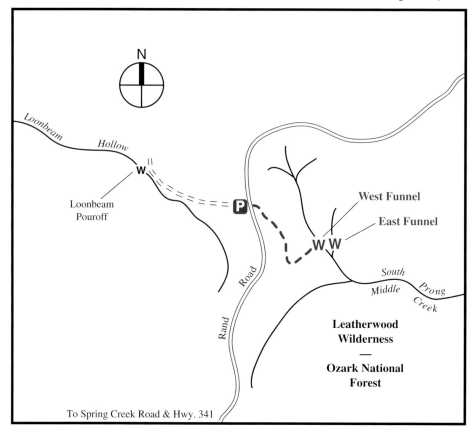

FUNNEL FALLS, East and West. *Wow*—this is one terrific spot, and pretty easy to get to! If you are a photographer, be sure to take plenty of film because you will need it. It is known as "the Funnel" because the rock formation at the East Falls funnels water down into it. The water action has created a natural stone arch.

From Big Flat, go 3.8 miles east on Hwy. 14 and TURN LEFT onto Hwy. 341 (paved). Go 2.3 miles and TURN LEFT onto Rand Road/FR#1118 (gravel). Go 6.5 miles to the intersection with Spring Creek Road and TURN RIGHT (still on Rand Road). Go .8 mile and PARK on the left, where a little jeep road takes off on that side of the road.

Cross the road and head straight down into the woods. You will soon come to an old road trace—TURN RIGHT and follow this road until it begins to swing sharply back to the right—there are many rock outcrops here so it will be easy to find. LEAVE THE ROAD there, TURN LEFT and head steeply down the hill on a faint trail. This will take you on down to the falls area (additional photos on the next pages). Be *extra careful* there because the rock formations could also "funnel" you into a fatal fall.

If you have the time, take the short, easy hike down the jeep road on the opposite side of the road from The Funnel (where you parked). It drops on down less than a half mile to an incredible viewpoint that looks out over the lower Buffalo River area. There is also a

West Funnel Falls

pouroff there. The flow is seldom enough to create a big waterfall, but the sheer height of the drop makes it impressive (more than 80 feet). The first time I visited it the wind was blowing so hard and coming in from out in front of the falls that the entire volume of water was blown back up and over the bluff! It was below freezing, and the bushes and trees above the falls were all coated with layers of ice—it was quite a sight.

Emergency contact: Marion County Sheriff, 870-449-4236

East Funnel Falls (the bottom part)

East Funnel Falls (the top part w/natural bridge)

Tassel Spring Falls – ★★★+ – 44′

.5 mile roundtrip, easy bushwhack, GPS helpful

Lat/Lon–36 04.535 N, 92 22.048 W • UTM–5 **56** 969 E, 39 **92** 308 N, Norfork SE Quad

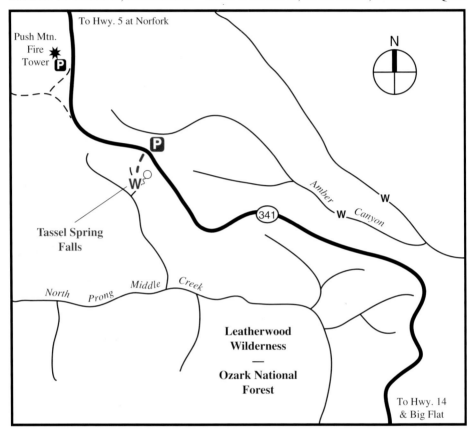

TASSEL SPRING FALLS. This is one of the more unusual waterfalls we have. The falls is not really all that great, but the moss "tassel" that grows there is very interesting. They say this tassel, which is actually a tangle of moss, roots, vines, and probably some dirt, used to grow nearly all the way to the ground. But vandals shot off the lower half of it, and now only about half of it remains. There is no trail, but the bushwhack down to the falls is short, although the climb back out is pretty steep. It's a quick stop on the way to or from the other waterfalls further up the road.

From Big Flat, go 3.8 miles east on Hwy. 14 and TURN LEFT onto Hwy. 341 (paved). Go 6.4 miles and PARK on the side of the road—look for a pulloff on the right.

Go across the highway and head steeply down the hill. You will come to the edge of the bluff soon. Look for the concrete basin that sits at the very top of the bluff—the tassel is attached to the base of a tree next to this basin, and the waterfall flows over the bluff and down the tassel. No swinging!

Emergency contact: Baxter County Sheriff, 870–425–6222

Tassel Spring Falls
(This is the top 25 feet of the moss "tassel" that used to hang all the way to near the ground—it's trying to grow back a little bit every day.)

Helen's Pouroff – ★★★★★ – 71′

5.4 miles roundtrip, medium hike/bushwhack, GPS required
Lat/Lon–36 05.813 N, 92 23.586 W • UTM–5 **54** 647 E, 39 **94** 656 N, Big Flat Quad

Woodsman Pouroff – ★★★★+ – 66′

Add 1.2 to above (6.6 total), medium hike/bushwhack, GPS required
Lat/Lon–36 05.862 N, 92 24.168 W • UTM–5 **53** 774 E, 39 **94** 741 N, Big Flat Quad

Cathedral Falls – ★★★★★ – 87′

Add .7 to above (7.3 total for all), medium-difficult hike/bushwhack
GPS required
Lat/Lon–36 06.199 N, 92 24.216 W • UTM–5 **53** 698 E, 39 **95** 363 N, Big Flat Quad

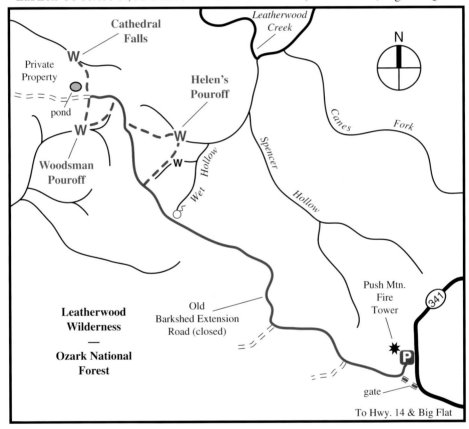

HELEN'S POUROFF/WOODSMAN POUROFF/CATHEDRAL FALLS. All three of these falls pour over tall bluffs and are well worth the extra effort to get to. The hike is along the old Barkshed Extension Road (closed to vehicles, except for property owners). It is easy hiking, but there are short bushwhacks required to each falls. A GPS is really a must here.

From Big Flat, go 3.8 miles east on Hwy. 14 and TURN LEFT onto Hwy. 341 (paved). Go 6.9 miles, TURN LEFT and PARK next to the base of Push Mountain Tower. (You can also park at gated Barkshed Extension Road on the left just before the tower, but there's not much room to park without blocking the gate.)

Helen's Pouroff

Head down the hill on the little horse trail that is next to the hitching post—TURN RIGHT once you get to the jeep road just below. Follow the road (stay RIGHT at the first fork) for 2.3 miles, then LEAVE THE ROAD to the RIGHT and drop down into a small drainage. This will take you down to a bluffline—TURN LEFT and follow the bluff. You may come to a nice 40 foot falls first, or arrive at Helen's Pouroff at 2.7 depending on where you hit the bluff. There are several large chunks of rock sitting on top of the bluff near the big falls, plus a little hole in the bluff that you can see down through. Some of the rocks are in the shape of a slice of pizza! This is named after Helen Elsner, who directed me to many of the waterfalls in "The Leatherwoods"—it is one of her favorites. Her book *The Buffalo River and Surrounding Watershed* is a great resource for many places up and down the Buffalo River area (research was all from horseback, with L.R. Alexander).

Woodsman Pouroff

From Helen's Pouroff hike back up to the jeep road and TURN RIGHT. Stay on the road for a little bit, then LEAVE THE ROAD to the LEFT and bushwhack down into the drainage that will take you to Woodsman Pouroff at 3.4. It was named after Gene "Jake the Woodsman" Boyd who has spent a lifetime exploring The Leatherwoods. There is a neat little cove of sorts in behind the waterfall that my wife, Pam, is standing in above. Every time she sees this picture she reminds me that there was a "critter of some sort" back in it!

From the top of this falls you can head up around to the left of the hill and follow an old road trace most of the way back up to the jeep road. TURN LEFT at the road and you will come to an opening which is private property. TURN RIGHT and follow the property line straight down the hillside, past a pond over on the left. Go all the way down to the

Cathedral Falls

creek (which is below the private property) and TURN LEFT and follow the creek just a little way to the top of Cathedral Falls at 3.9. To get to the bottom of the falls, cross the creek and follow the bluffline to the right for .25 mile or so (some great views down into the Leatherwood Creek Valley) until you can find a way down through it, then hike along the base of the bluff back to the falls. There are some giant pine trees in here, and the bluffline is quite spectacular—reminded me of a great wilderness cathedral.

To return to the parking area, simply make your way back up to the jeep road, TURN LEFT and follow it all the way back—a hike of just over 3.0 miles. None of the hiking is all that difficult, but it does make for a very long day.

Emergency contact: Baxter County Sheriff, 870–425–6222

Dewey Canyon Falls – ★★★★★ – 88′

.4 miles roundtrip, easy bushwhack, GPS not needed

Lat/Lon–36 05.435 N, 92 20.843 W • UTM–5 **58** 767 E, 39 **93** 984 N, Norfork SE Quad

Bumpers Falls (2) – ★★★★★ – 27′/71′

Same as above, easy bushwhack, GPS not needed

Lat/Lon–36 05.417 N, 92 20.859 W • UTM–5 **58** 744 E, 39 **93** 949 N, Norfork SE Quad

Heuston Falls – ★★★★+ – 54′

Add .4 to above, easy bushwhack, GPS not needed

Lat/Lon–36 05.464 N, 92 21.019 W • UTM–5 **58** 503 E, 39 **94** 036 N, Norfork SE Quad

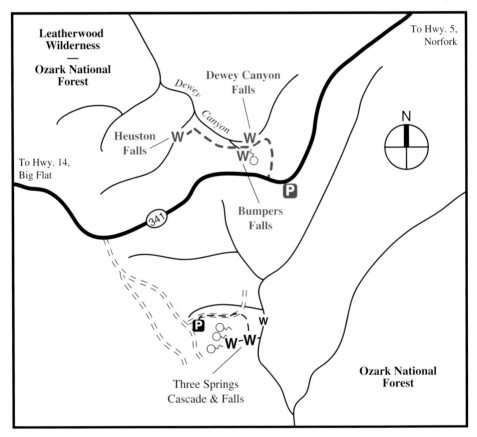

DEWEY CANYON/BUMPERS/HEUSTON FALLS. Here are four great waterfalls just a stone's throw off the highway. Like many of the falls in this area they look best when the water is really high.

From Big Flat, go 3.8 miles east on Hwy. 14 and TURN LEFT onto Hwy. 341 (paved). Go 8.9 miles and PARK on the right at the beginning of the big curve.

CROSS the road and go back to the left to the beginning of a guard rail. You will find a faint trail there that heads down into the drainage to a little creek. TURN LEFT and follow the creek just a short distance to the top of Dewey Canyon Falls.

Dewey Canyon Falls

From the top of Dewey Canyon Falls TURN LEFT and follow the bluffline and you will come to the Upper Bumpers Falls (turn page for photo). The bluffline actually splits, or should I say a second bluffline rises up above. There is a spring up there that pours off the upper bluffline and creates this upper falls, then the water continues over the lower, taller bluff creating the lower falls. This is all close together and easy to see. You can get behind the upper falls and look back and see both Bumpers Falls and Dewey Canyon Falls at the same time. Bumpers Falls is named after our former governor and United States Senator from Arkansas, Dale Bumpers. He wrote the forward to the very first guidebook that I ever

Lower Dale Bumpers Falls (Dewey Canyon Falls visible in background)

did (Ozark Highlands Trail Guide). Besides doing a great deal for the state of Arkansas, he was a tireless supporter of wilderness and other conservation issues his entire career.

To get to Heuston Falls CONTINUE along the top of the bluffline and it will curve back to the left and come to the top of the falls. John Heuston has been one of the driving forces behind the Ozark Society for several decades. He fought in those early years to save the Buffalo River and to establish our wilderness areas. He is an eloquent outdoor writer and a great story teller.

Emergency contact: Baxter County Sheriff, 870-425-6222

**Upper
Dale Bumpers Falls**

John Heuston Falls

Ozarks Region Waterfalls
(outside the Buffalo River drainage)

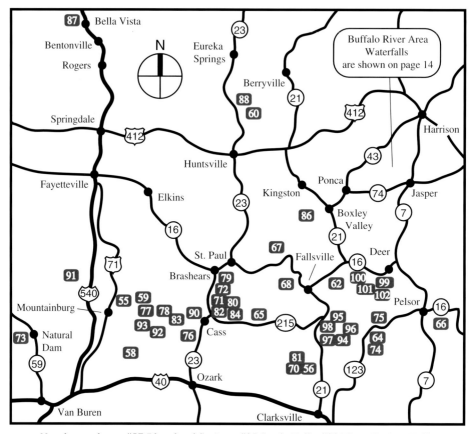

Not shown above: #57 Blanchard Springs, #85 Steele Falls, #89 Three Springs Falls. All three are located near the community of Fiftysix in Stone County, north of Hwy. 14 and east of Hwy. 341.

"Ozark" is the word for "waterfall" used by some of the wandering Nomad tribes in the Sahara Desert. Just kidding, but it does seem like there are more waterfalls in the Ozarks than just about anyplace else in the central United States. We have two raw materials here in great abundance—water and bluffs—and when combined the two produce, what else— *waterfalls*. During the rainy season you can probably hike up just about any drainage in the Ozarks and find a waterfall of some sort. I have picked out some of the best that I know of—and that others have told me about—to include in this section. Some of them are located in the middle of nowhere and require a serious and often difficult trek to get to, while others are right next to the road and offer easy access. And just in case you have not read the first part of this guidebook yet and were wondering where the famous Buffalo River waterfalls are listed—they have their own section (see page 14).

Fall #	Name	Beauty Rating	Height	Hike Difficulty	Page #
55	Artist Point Falls	★★★★	15	Medium	180
56	Aspen Falls	★★★★	37	Difficult	132
94	Bear Skull Falls	★★★★	22	Medium	128
57	Blanchard Springs	★★★★	10	Easy	110
58	Devils Canyon Falls	★★★★★	63	Difficult	178
95	Discovery Falls	★★★★	43	Difficult	128
59	Dockery Gap Falls	★★★★★	36	Difficult	176
60	Eagle's Nest Falls	★★★★	41	Easy	148
61	Forever Falls	★★★★★	47	Difficult	118
99	French Falls	★★★★+	47	Medium	136
62	Glory Hole	★★★★★	31	Medium	140
63	Graves Canyon (2)	★★★★	31/35	Difficult	118
64	Haw Creek Falls	★★★	6	Easy	122
65	High Bank Twins	★★★★★	71	Easy	162
96	Hobo Falls (2)	★★★★	23/27	Medium	126
100	Home Valley Falls	★★★★+	53	Difficult	136
66	Kings Bluff Falls	★★★★★	114	Easy	114
67	Kings River Falls	★★★★★	10	Easy	144
101	Latin Pouroff	★★★★+	74	Difficult	136
68	Lichen Falls	★★★★	28	Easy	142
69	Longpool Falls	★★★★+	44	Easy	116
70	Lucy Falls	★★★★	17	Medium	132
71	Mountain Fork Falls	★★★+	13	Difficult	156
72	Murray Falls	★★★★★	37	Medium	152
73	Natural Dam	★★★+	8x187	Easy	184
74	Pack Rat Falls	★★★★	24	Medium	122
75	Pam's Grotto	★★★★+	37	Medium	124
76	Pig Trail Falls	★★★	18	Easy	164
77	Rattlesnake Falls	★★★★	29	Easy	174
78	Robinson Falls (2)	★★★+	17/21	Medium	168
79	Senyard Falls	★★★★+	29	Medium	152
80	Sixty Foot Falls	★★★★+	56	Difficult	156
97	Slot Rock	★★★+	8	Medium	128
81	Spainhour Falls	★★★★	16	Medium	132
82	Spirit Mountain Falls	★★★+	15	Difficult	156
83	Spirits Creek Falls	★★★★	8	Medium	168
84	Spy Rock Falls	★★★	19	Easy	160
85	Steele Falls	★★★★★	66	Medium	112
98	Sunset Falls	★★★★	70	Difficult	128
86	Sweden Creek Falls	★★★★★	81	Medium	146
87	Tanyard Creek Falls	★★★+	12	Easy	186
88	Tea Kettle Falls	★★★★★	46	Medium	150
102	Tea Table Falls (2)	★★★★★	21/51	Difficult	136
89	Three Springs Falls (2)	★★★★	14/45	Easy	108
90	Train Trestle Falls	★★★★	31	Medium	166
91	Twin Falls at Devil's Den	★★★★	47/56	Easy	182
92	White Rock Cascade	★★★+	10	Medium	172
93	White Rock Falls	★★★★	31	Medium	172

Three Springs Cascade/Falls–★★★★–14′/45′

.6 mile roundtrip, easy hike, GPS helpful

Lat/Lon–36 04.990 N, 92 20.815 W • UTM–5 **58** 814 E, 39 **93** 160 N, Norfork SE Quad

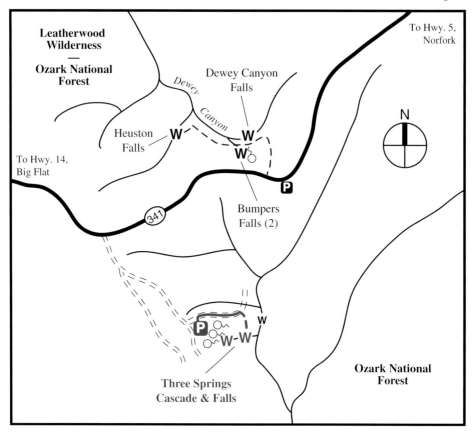

THREE SPRINGS CASCADE & FALLS. There are two little springs and one large spring that all run together to form a waterfall. And there is a nice cascade that is just below the big spring that is worth a look too. Both are easy to get to right off the highway.

From Big Flat, go 3.8 miles east on Hwy. 14 and TURN LEFT onto Hwy. 341 (paved). Go 8.3 miles and TURN RIGHT onto a jeep road (used to be Cook Road). Bear LEFT at the first fork, and then TURN LEFT at the bottom of the next hill and PARK in a clearing (this is a wildlife food plot), about .4 from the highway. The last run down to the food plot may be rough, but most vehicles should be able to make it.

Follow the jeep road that goes down the hill on the LEFT side of the food plot, and where it levels out a bit and curves back to the left TURN RIGHT onto a four-wheeler trail. This will take you over above the waterfall, which is just down on your LEFT, and to the base of the cascade, which will be up on your right. All of this only .3 from the food plot. If you follow the bluffline at the top of the falls back to the left you will come to another waterfall (23 feet tall), which has some interesting rock formations around it. OR you could follow the bluffline around to the right from the top of the falls and you will eventually find a way down into the canyon to see both falls.

Emergency contact: Baxter County Sheriff, 870–425–6222

Three Springs Cascade

Three Springs Falls

Blanchard Springs – ★★★★ – 10'

.25 mile roundtrip, easy stroll, GPS not needed

Lat/Lon–35 57.549 N, 92 10.544 W • UTM–5 **74** 344 E, 39 **79** 523 N, Fiftysix Quad

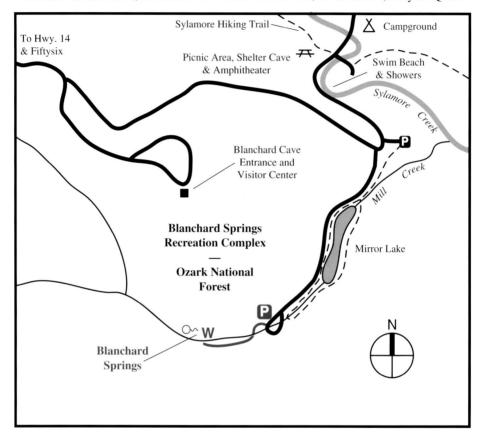

BLANCHARD SPRINGS. Some people might not consider this a waterfall, but it is such a delightful spot I just had to include it. It is a magical place that has attracted visitors for many generations. Plus, the spring and falls run all summer long, so you can always go there for a refreshing moment on a hot day.

I worked at Blanchard Cave as a tour guide from 1973–1976 and used to visit this spot often after work, just to relax and watch the water. I must relate this funny story that happened one summer there. I was allowed to make a trip through the lower level of the cave with two of the three guys who originally explored and mapped the watercourse. You have to scuba dive most of the way, and with zero visibility, once you muddy up the water it is extremely hazardous (only five people that I know of have ever made the trip). If something happens to your equipment, you are in big trouble because you cannot simply "surface." The river pops up into several dry rooms along the way, and they contain some of the most incredible cave formations that I have ever seen. Anyway, it was a hot summer weekend and there were probably 100 people gathered around the entrance of the spring when we came popping out. You are not allowed to enter this spring, much less scuba dive through the cave. But here we came, all wearing wet suits with all sorts of strange gear dangling from us. I guess many of the visitors thought we were creatures from the Black

Blanchard Springs

Lagoon or something because dozens of them went running in all directions, screaming for help. We were laughing so hard we nearly choked on our mouthpieces!

The turnoff to Blanchard Springs is located just east of the community of Fiftysix (between Big Flat and Sylamore on Hwy. 14). There are many thousands of visitors a year to this place so everything is well marked. Just follow the signs to the parking area for the spring, then take the boardwalk along the creek to the mouth of the spring. This is one waterfall where you can bring your baby along in a stroller! My recommendation is that you plan to visit during the winter when you will have the place to yourself. Tour the cave and spend the night in the campground, then go see the spring early the next morning—sometimes when it is cold you can see mist coming from the spring.

Emergency contact: Stone County Sheriff, 870–269–2700

Steele Falls – ★★★★★ – 66'

3.2 miles roundtrip, easy-medium hike, GPS not needed

Lat/Lon–36 01.037 N, 92 10.778 W • UTM–5 **73** 938 E, 39 **85** 967 N, Calico Rock Quad

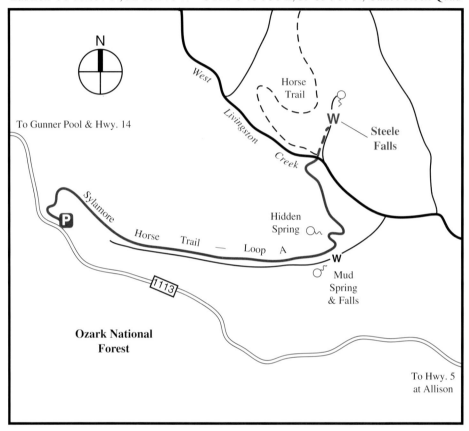

STEELE FALLS. The Sylamore District of the Ozark National Forest is known for its many springs. One of them produces this wonderful waterfall that is located along part of the main horse trail in the area. It is an easy hike to get down to, but is a bit of a climb coming out.

To get to the parking area, first go to the town of Fiftysix (located between Big Flat and Sylamore on Hwy. 14), then go west on Hwy. 14 about a mile and TURN RIGHT onto FR#1102 (gravel). This is the road to Gunner Pool Campground and will be well marked. Go 5.8 miles (past Gunner Pool Campground) and TURN RIGHT onto FR#1113. You are now actually on part of the horse trail that follows this road. Go 1.0 and PARK on the left.

The horse trail (Sylamore Horse Trail, Hidden Springs/Loop A) follows an old forest service road from this point on and is no longer open to vehicle traffic—get on the horse trail and follow it down the hill. It is a lovely gentle hike through open forest. Soon you will pass a nice waterfall off the trail to the right—it is just out of sight but if the water is running you will be able to hear it. It's called Mud Spring Falls, and is 39 feet tall.

Just beyond this point the trail swings to the left and switchbacks down the hill a couple of times. Near the bottom of the hill it curves to the right and comes to West Livingston Creek. WADE THE CREEK and then LEAVE THE ROAD to the RIGHT and head up into the woods on a narrow volunteer trail. This little trail follows a smaller stream right on up to the base of Steele Falls at 1.6.

Jim Steele Falls

This falls is named after Jim Steele, a forest service guy I worked with 30 years ago on this ranger district. He has been responsible for trail development in the district, and for the management of Leatherwood Wilderness. One time he rode way back into the wilderness on horseback, cut up an old car body that was an eyesore, and carried it out piece by piece on pack horses. I guess he was sticking to the letter of the law that says no vehicles are allowed in wilderness areas!

By the way, the last time I was at this waterfall I lost my prized felt hat that had become my trademark—let me know if you find it ($2 reward offered!).

Emergency contact: Stone County Sheriff, 870–269–2700

Kings Bluff Falls – ★★★★★ – 114′

1.9 mile loop, easy hike, GPS not needed

Lat/Lon–35 43.488 N, 93 01.507 W • UTM–4 **97** 744 E, 39 **53** 217 N, Sand Gap Quad

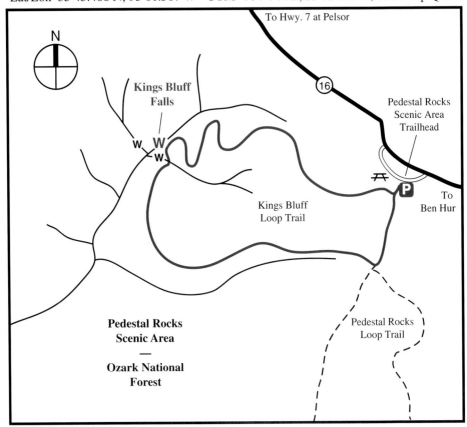

KINGS BLUFF FALLS. This is one of the tallest waterfalls in Arkansas, and it is a beauty! It is located in the Pedestal Rocks Scenic Area, and the trail to it is one of two loops that visit the area. The bluffline there is quite grand, with many interesting geological formations, including stone features sculpted over time by wind and rocks. The big bluffs make for a dangerous situation, especially for younger folks, so be sure to keep a hand on them if you take them along. There is a railing along the top of the tallest bluff at the waterfall, but it would be easy for someone to get over it so *be careful!*

To get to the trailhead, take Hwy. 16 east from Pelsor on Hwy. 7 (Pelsor is located between Russellville and Jasper). Go about 6.0 miles and look for the sign to the RIGHT. If you get to Ben Hur, you've gone too far, so just turn around and go back about 2.5 miles. There is a picnic table and restroom at the trailhead, but camping is not allowed.

As soon as you head out on the trail and go across the stone bridge TURN RIGHT and head out on the Kings Bluff Trail (the trail straight ahead goes out to Pedestal Rocks—we will join it on the way back). This first part of the trail is actually an old road that heads up the hill just a little bit, then levels out and swings to the left. It begins to drop on down the hillside and becomes just a plain hiking trail. After several switchbacks you will come right out onto the top of Kings Bluff at the 1.0 point. This is one spectacular spot, so plan to stick around a while.

Kings Bluff Falls

This waterfall will run much of the wet season, but for a real treat try to get here after a big rain. You may see other waterfalls in the valley below too. A very nice area! Be sure to save some film though, because the next section of bluffline is quite scenic. The trail continues along the top of the bluff to the LEFT, past deep crevices and scenic views. It eventually comes to the end of the bluff, then makes its way gradually up through the forest and intersects with the Pedestal Rocks Loop at 1.8—TURN LEFT and follow the trail back to the trailhead. (Turn right for the 2.6 mile loop out to Pedestal Rocks.)

Emergency contact: Pope County Sheriff, 479–967–9300

Longpool Falls – ★★★★+ – 44′

1.5 miles roundtrip, easy hike, GPS not needed

Lat/Lon–35 32.958 N, 93 09.126 W • UTM–4 **86** 230 E, 39 **33** 764 N, Treat Quad

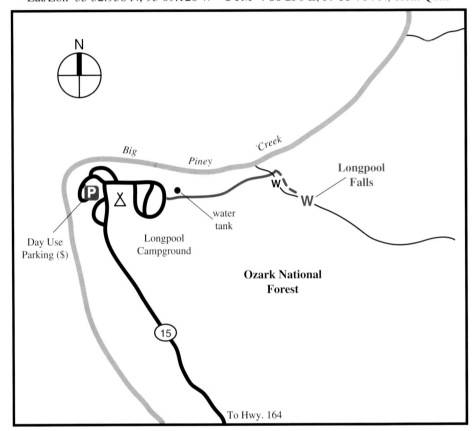

LONGPOOL FALLS. This waterfall is located right next to a very popular recreation area, but few folks ever go see it. The hike to the falls is easy, and the water coming over the bluff is quite powerful, especially since it comes from a very small drainage above. There is a big swimming hole at the recreation area, a picnic area, quite a few campsites, and nice restrooms. The place will be crowded on spring weekends and the river filled with canoeists as this is also one of the main access points for the river. Waterfall season is the same as floating season, and we all want high water! There is a day use fee charged to park here, and the parking area is on the opposite side of the area from where we begin our hike.

To get to Longpool Recreation Area, head north on Hwy. 7 from Dover (north of Russellville). TURN LEFT onto Hwy. 164, and then TURN RIGHT onto CR#14 (old Hwy. 7) at the sign. This road becomes CR#15, which ends at Longpool, 4.8 miles from Hwy. 164 (it is all paved). To get to the PARKING AREA, go past the pay station and follow the main road around to the LEFT, then PARK in the big lot.

From the parking area, head on over to the Loop B Camp Area, and go all the way to the back. There is an old road trace that takes off from the main road in between campsites #14 & #9. Take this roadbed up past an old water tank, then continue uphill just a little bit. The roadbed soon tops out and begins to head downhill. You are hiking upstream along Big Piney Creek which you can see down on your left. Big Piney is one of the most

Longpool Falls

beautiful and popular floating streams in the Ozarks. The roadbed comes on down to river level where you come to a creek—there is a nice little waterfall just up to your right here that should be running well. The big falls is up behind that one—cross the stream, TURN RIGHT, and head up past the little falls. You'll have to do a bit of boulder scrambling so be careful, but you will soon hear the thunder and see this hidden beauty.

Emergency contact: Pope County Sheriff, 479–967–9300

Forever Falls – ★★★★★ – 47′

2.0 miles roundtrip, difficult bushwhack, GPS recommended
Lat/Lon–35 35.513 N, 93 11.349 W • UTM–4 **82** 880 E, 39 **38** 491 N, Treat Quad

Graves Canyon Falls (2) – ★★★★ – 31′/35′

Same area as above, difficult bushwhack, GPS recommended
Lat/Lon–35 35.702 N, 93 11.192 W • UTM–4 **83** 118 E, 39 **38** 840 N, Treat Quad

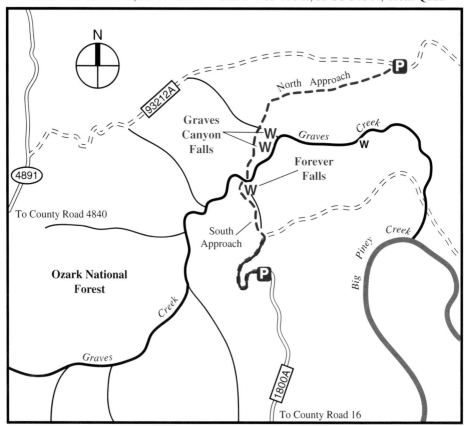

FOREVER FALLS/GRAVES CANYON FALLS. Here is a wonderful canyon tucked into a side pocket of the Big Piney River. These falls are difficult to get to (easier with a *serious* 4wd), but well worth the trip if you can make it. You will want to stay here forever! One kayaker that I know calls this the most scenic wild run in the Ozarks.

North Approach. From Hwy. 123, go 3.9 miles south of Haw Creek Campground (.6 south of FR#1003 turn) and TURN LEFT onto CR#4840 (gravel). Go 9.8 miles (past Pilot Knob) and TURN LEFT onto CR#4891 (or *turn right* for the south approach to get to FR#1800-A). Go 1.7 miles (the road # may change) and TURN RIGHT onto log road #93212A. This is a *rough* 4wd road with pending timber sales. You can PARK anytime after 1.8 miles—the road runs along the top edge of the ridge, with the canyon being down on the right, way down. (If you have a *serious* 4wd you may be able to drive all the way to the bottom.) Park and head south (downhill) into the woods. If you have a GPS, simply make a beeline towards the falls. If not, make your way down the hillside any way that you choose to the creek below. Either way the going will be tough, down a *very steep* hillside.

Forever Falls

Once you get to the creek you will need to look around a bit in order to find the falls. It's a mile hike or less from the road to the creek, give or take.

The lower two falls are on the north side of the creek (turn page for photos), right next to each other in the middle of a narrow canyon that is flanked by 20–30 foot tall bluffs—if you get down into this winding canyon you may not be able to get back out for a while! Forever Falls is on the south side of the creek at the upper end of the canyon, several hundred yards upstream from the other falls, located in a hairpin curve.

South Approach. This parking spot will get you closer (especially if you have a 4wd), but if the water is really high you will end up on the wrong side of the river to view the waterfalls and may not be able to cross the creek. From Dover take Hwy. 7 north and

Graves Canyon Falls (upstream falls)

TURN LEFT onto Hwy. 164. Go past the turn to Longpool and cross the Big Piney River, then TURN RIGHT onto CR#16/Pilot Knob Road (gravel). Go 4.5 miles and TURN RIGHT onto FR#1800–A. (You can also reach 1800–A from Hwy. 123—go 9.8 miles on CR#4840 and TURN RIGHT onto CR#4891/CR#16, go about 3.3 miles, then TURN LEFT onto FR#1800–A.) This is a good road for the first 1.6 miles—park there if you have a normal vehicle. (A *serious* 4wd can continue on down the jeep trail, even all the way to the river if you are adventurous.) Continue down the jeep road on foot as it swings to the left

Graves Canyon Falls (downstream falls)

downhill and makes a big switchback to the right. Eventually the jeep road will level out some (watch out for a pending timber sale in the area). Somewhere in here leave the road TO THE LEFT and strike off through the woods downhill. It will be a lot easier to navigate with a GPS. This hillside is not as difficult as the North Approach, but it does get steep as you get close to the creek. Once you find the creek you will simply have to explore around to find the falls. The hike down to the creek is a little less than a mile.

Emergency contact: Pope County Sheriff, 479–967–9300

Haw Creek Falls – ★★★ – 6'

Drive to within 100 feet of the falls, GPS not needed

Lat/Lon–35 40.669 N, 93 15.312 W • UTM–4 **76** 921 E, 39 **48** 036 N, Rosetta Quad

Pack Rat Falls – ★★★★ – 24'

.5 mile roundtrip, easy-medium bushwhack, GPS not needed

Lat/Lon–35 40.360 N, 93 15.201 W • UTM–4 **77** 087 E, 39 **47** 464 N, Rosetta Quad

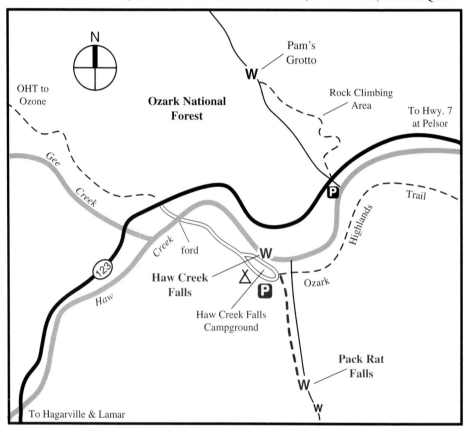

HAW CREEK FALLS. You can drive to within 100 feet of this falls, which is located at the edge of one of my favorite campsites in the Ozarks (picnic tables, toilets, water). The falls aren't very tall or impressive, but make a refreshing stop if you are touring in the area. I like to lie out on the rock slab at night and count falling stars. Haw Creek Falls Campground is located on Hwy. 123 between Lamar (near Clarksville) and Pelsor (on Hwy. 7)—watch for the sign on the highway. The gravel road into the campground fords Haw Creek. Look out for high water and don't drive or hike across if there is flooding.

PACK RAT FALLS. There is a hidden canyon that comes out next to the campground where you will find this falls. It is a magical little place, filled with moss-covered rocks, tumbling water, and wildflowers. Simply go to the back of the campground and follow the little creek upstream to the RIGHT. Watch out for slippery rocks! You will come to the falls within .25 mile. There is a second nice falls just upstream, but it requires a bit more scrambling up and over steep hillsides to get to.

Emergency contact: Johnson County Sheriff, 479–754–2200

Haw Creek Falls (above), **Pack Rat Falls** (below)

Pam's Grotto – ★★★★+ – 37′

1.0 mile roundtrip, medium hike/bushwhack, GPS not needed

Lat/Lon–35 40.998 N, 93 15.323 W • UTM–4 **76** 906 E, 39 **48** 644 N, Rosetta Quad

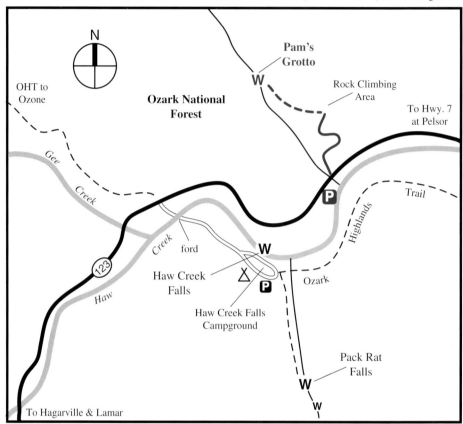

PAM'S GROTTO. I first stumbled onto this beautiful spot in 1982 while looking for a possible route of the Ozark Highlands Trail through the area. I knew it was a very special place then. The next time I saw the falls I was with my future bride, Pam, who the falls is named after. We were working with a group of 60 volunteers from the Petra Rock Climbing Gym in Springfield, MO, and helped them build the short, but steep trail up to a rock climbing area. You will see those towering bluffs as you make your way to Pam's Grotto.

Take Hwy. 123 to Haw Creek Campground (located between Lamar and Pelsor near the Big Piney River), then go .5 mile east on Hwy. 123 from the turnoff to the campground. There is a pulloff that drops down to a small parking area on the RIGHT—park there (you will be next to Haw Creek). The trail begins *across* the road and to the right of the small creek that comes out of the forest and goes under the highway.

Follow the trail up the hill about .25 mile to the base of the big bluffs. TURN LEFT and follow along the base of the bluffs and you will come right into the Grotto after about .5 mile total. You will be hiking along admiring the bluff and all of a sudden there it will be! The waterfall itself is guarded by a house-sized boulder. It is a small area with a giant personality, and really looks good with a lot of water.

Emergency contact: Johnson County Sheriff, 479–754–2200

Pam's Grotto

Hobo Falls (2) – ★★★★ – 23'/27'

3.0 miles roundtrip, medium hike, GPS not required

Lat/Lon–35 40.854 N, 93 20.040 W • UTM–4 **69** 792 E, 39 **48** 399 N, Rosetta Quad

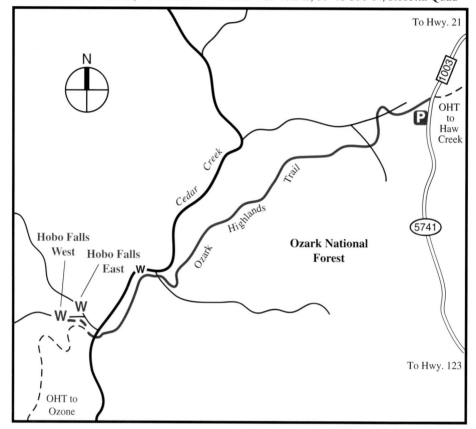

HOBO FALLS. Most folks walk right on past the neat little canyon that holds these two waterfalls. They are definitely worth a look, especially when there is lots of water. Over the years we have found the remnants of a hobo camp several different times in the area, even one right under the bluffline next to these waterfalls—hence the name.

To get to the parking area from the community of Ozone, take Hwy. 21 north 6.7 miles & TURN RIGHT onto CR#5570/FR#1003 (becomes CR#5680 & then CR#5741). Go 10.1 miles & park where the Ozark Highlands Trail crosses the road. **OR** from Haw Creek Camp, take Hwy. 123 south 3.3 miles & TURN RIGHT onto CR#5741/FR#1003 & go 4.7 miles.

The Ozark Highlands Trail takes off to the west, drops down the hill, crossing a couple of small streams, and eventually makes its way down to and alongside Cedar Creek. There is a wonderful slough area at 1.1 that ends with a small pouroff into an emerald pool (too shallow to dive into!). This is a very fragile area, and if you camp here, be sure to camp *away* from the pool area. The trail continues downstream, and crosses Cedar Creek at 1.4.

As you continue on the trail you will see a side canyon just ahead and on the RIGHT— leave the trail and follow the canyon just a couple hundred feet upstream. The East Falls will be visible on your right in a second side canyon, and the West Falls will be straight ahead another 100 yards or so. Be sure to save some energy for the climb out!

Emergency contact: Johnson County Sheriff, 479–754–2200

Hobo Falls East

Hobo Falls West

Bear Skull Falls – ★★★★ – 22′

3.0 miles roundtrip, medium hike, GPS helpful

Lat/Lon–35 40.192 N, 93 21.732 W • UTM–4 **67** 236 E, 39 **47** 185 N, Rosetta Quad

Slot Rock – ★★★+ – 8′

4.4 miles roundtrip (includes above), medium hike, GPS helpful

Lat/Lon–35 40.560 N, 93 21.791 W • UTM–4 **67** 148 E, 39 **47** 865 N, Rosetta Quad

Sunset Falls – ★★★★ – 70′

5.8 miles roundtrip (includes above), medium bushwhack, GPS recommended

Lat/Lon–35 40.591 N, 93 21.214 W • UTM–4 **68** 019 E, 39 **47** 918 N, Rosetta Quad

Discovery Falls – ★★★★ – 43′

6.4 miles roundtrip (includes all of the above), difficult bushwhack, GPS recommended

Lat/Lon–35 40.622 N, 93 21.175 W • UTM–4 **68** 078 E, 39 **47** 977 N, Rosetta Quad

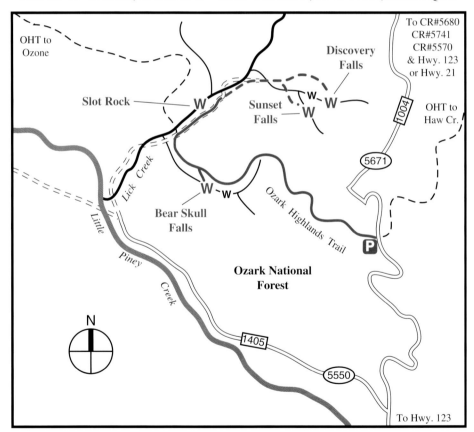

BEAR SKULL/SLOT ROCK/SUNSET/DISCOVERY FALLS. Spend a day in this area and visit four waterfalls with very different personalities. One is tall and skinny, another barely a waterfall at all but a wonderful swimming hole, a third is a typical Ozark waterfall along the Ozark Highlands Trail (OHT), and finally a surprise—a beautiful waterfall high up in

Bear Skull Falls

a hanging valley that I discovered one day while frantically looking for a direct way back to my car as darkness overtook me.

To get to the parking area from the community of Ozone, take Hwy. 21 north 6.7 miles and TURN RIGHT onto CR#5570/FR#1003 (it becomes CR#5680). Go 6.9 miles and TURN RIGHT onto CR#5671/FR#1004. Go 5.1 miles and PARK where the OHT crosses the road. **OR** from Haw Creek Campground, take Hwy. 123 south 3.3 miles and TURN RIGHT onto CR#5741/FR#1003 (becomes CR#5680) and go about 7.7 miles and TURN LEFT onto CR#5671/FR#1004. Go 5.1 miles and PARK where the OHT crosses the road.

Get on the OHT and take it to the west from the parking area. It will work around a hillside and down into a big drainage, eventually coming to Bear Skull Falls at 1.5 (there is a short blue-blazed spur trail that goes over to the base of it). From there the trail continues down the hill on an old road all the way to the bottom of the hill and hits a jeep road. The OHT continues straight across the road at this point, but you want to TURN RIGHT and hike along the jeep road about .2 and you will come to Slot Rock down on the LEFT.

Slot Rock (above), **Sunset Falls** (below)

Discovery Falls

From Slot Rock continue along the jeep road upstream, then begin to bushwhack upstream when the road crosses the creek (you don't cross the creek). Follow the main creek until you come to a side creek coming in from the right (the jeep road has rejoined you now). TURN RIGHT and head up this side creek—it will take you to Sunset Falls if you bear right at the fork (the last part is *really* steep). The left fork goes up to another nice falls that is not pictured (19' tall). Above that falls is Discovery Falls, but you have to get up on top of the bluff to get to it.

From the 19' falls, follow the bluffline back to the LEFT a couple of hundred yards and find a way up to the top of the bluff. Then TURN RIGHT and make your way *care-fully* around to Discovery Falls. It's a 3.1 mile trip back out, a tough uphill hike.

Emergency contact: Johnson County Sheriff, 479–754–2200

Spainhour Falls – ★★★★ – 16'

7.2 miles roundtrip (if you hike), medium hike, GPS helpful
Lat/Lon–35 37.299 N, 93 27.901 W • UTM–4 **57** 904 E, 39 **41** 876 N, Ludwig Quad

Lucy Falls – ★★★★ – 17'

Add .6 to above, medium bushwhack, GPS recommended
Lat/Lon–35 36.736 N, 93 27.575 W • UTM–4 **58** 392 E, 39 **40** 833 N, Ludwig Quad

Aspen Falls – ★★★★ – 37'

Add .4 to above, medium bushwhack, GPS recommended
Lat/Lon–35 36.797 N, 93 27.432 W • UTM–4 **58** 608 E, 39 **40** 944 N, Ludwig Quad

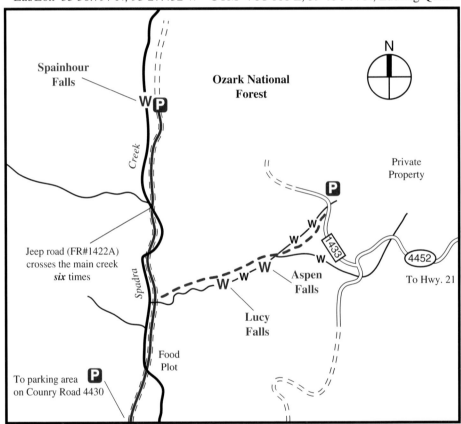

SPAINHOUR/LUCY/ASPEN FALLS. When we went to visit the locals' favorite Spainhour Falls, we took a little detour on the way back and discovered a narrow gorge filled with waterfalls. Our pups, Aspen and Lucy, had a big trip that day, and they are the ones that led us up into the gorge, so I have named a couple of the falls after them. The normal way into this area is to drive/hike along a jeep road. The road is pretty rough, and crosses the creek six times, so when the water is high this route isn't a real possibility for driving. During normal water flow you can probably get all the way to the falls if you have a *serious* 4wd and don't mind the abuse, thus saving you the 7.2-mile hike. Most folks that I know simply park at the county road and hike in, making a day of it. If the water is really high, or you want an

Spainhour Falls

extreme challenge, there is another way in, which requires a *steep and difficult* bushwhack. There are additional waterfalls along the way, but it is a really tough trip, and only recommended for the seasoned bushwhacker who doesn't mind a broken ankle or two.

To get to the main route take Hwy. 21 north from Clarksville 6.3 miles and TURN LEFT onto CR#4400 (paved). (7.7 miles south of the Ozone Post Office.) This is the road to Zion Church, and the turn is just north of a little store on Hwy. 21. Go 2.0 miles and TURN RIGHT onto FR#1430 (paved, then gravel). Go .6 miles and TURN LEFT onto CR#4418 (this turn is right after the road becomes CR#4451). Go 1.0 miles and TURN RIGHT onto CR#4420/FR#1422. Go .6 miles andTURN RIGHT onto CR#4430, then go .2 miles and TURN LEFT onto FR#1422A (jeep road) and PARK (or continue in your 4wd).

Hike/drive on this road for a total of 3.6 miles as it follows Spadra Creek upstream, crossing it six times, and you will find the falls down on the left. At the second crossing of the creek around 1.2 there may be a neat waterfall pouring off the bluff on the other side. After the fourth crossing at 2.4 there is a wildlife food plot on the right. The next side creek that you come to after this (it comes in from the right or east) is the creek that leads up into the gorge that is filled with waterfalls—TURN RIGHT and bushwhack up the creek to Lucy and Aspen Falls (about .5 up to Aspen—turn the page for photos). This is also the creek that you would come down if bushwhacking in from the difficult route.

To reach the parking spot for the alternate bushwhack into the falls, CONTINUE on Hwy. 21 north from the Hwy. 76 turnoff another 5.0 miles (2.7 miles south of Ozone) and TURN LEFT onto CR#4452. Go 1.3 miles and TURN RIGHT onto FR#1433 at the fork in the road. Go .3 and PARK just past a little creek crossing. You may be able to look out from the road on that last little bit of the drive and see big bluffs way down in there—that is where you are headed, and those bluffs are just above Aspen Falls.

133

Lucy Falls

From the parking spot you will want to hike down that little creek you just crossed—it drops off in a big hurry, and is an *extremely* steep and difficult bushwhack and not for the inexperienced or faint of heart. But when the water is running it is a spectacular gorge filled with boulders and lots of whitewater. You will pass a couple of waterfalls—one a pretty good-sized one—cross a four-wheeler trail, then intersect with a second creek coming down from your left (on the way back out you may want to take this fork—it comes out up on top on the road that you came in on, near where the road forks).

Aspen Falls (photo was taken when it was almost dark!)

From the intersection of the two creeks, just keep on heading down the gorge, and soon you will come to the top of Aspen Falls at .5, and the big bluffline that is up on the right. Keep on going past another waterfall, and then Lucy Falls. It is all fabulous scenery! You will finally hit bottom around the .9 mark and land on the jeep road—TURN RIGHT and follow the jeep road, crossing Spadra Creek twice, and Spainhour Falls will be on your left at 1.8. Good luck on the bushwhack out!

Emergency contact: Johnson County Sheriff, 479–754–2200

Tea Table Falls (2) – ★★★★★ – 21′/51′

2.0 miles roundtrip, medium bushwhack, GPS helpful

Lat/Lon–35 48.973 N, 93 16.779 W • UTM–4 **74** 753 E, 39 **63** 391 N, Swain Quad

Latin Pouroff – ★★★★+ – 74′

Add .6 to above, medium/difficult bushwhack, GPS helpful

Lat/Lon–35 49.066 N, 93 16.971 W • UTM–4 **74** 463 E, 39 **63** 563 N, Swain Quad

Home Valley Falls – ★★★★+ – 53′

Add .8 (3.4 total roundtrip), difficult bushwhack, GPS helpful

Lat/Lon–35 49.097 N, 93 17.260 W • UTM–4 **74** 029 E, 39 **63** 622 N, Swain Quad

French Falls – ★★★★+ – 47′

Add .5 (3.9 total roundtrip), easy/medium bushwhack, GPS helpful

Lat/Lon–35 48.955 N, 93 16.495 W • UTM–4 **75** 180 E, 39 **63** 356 N, Swain Quad

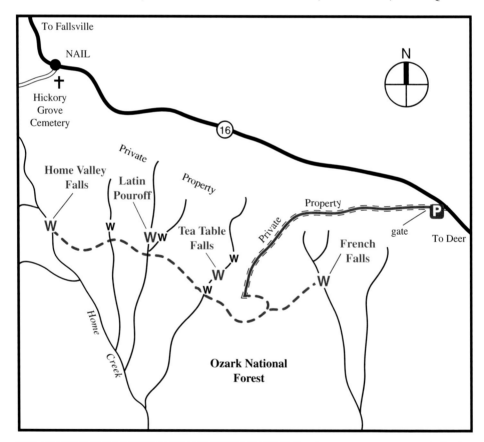

TEA TABLE/LATIN/HOME VALLEY/FRENCH FALLS. There are several waterfalls that pour over Home Valley Bluff—one of the greatest blufflines in the Ozarks. Most of the bluff is privately owned, so access has been scarce in the past. We now have permission from the landowner to access these wonderful waterfalls. He is Edd French, and owns Buffalo River Realty in Jasper (none of the bluff is for sale!). Tell him hi, thanks, and buy

Upper Tea Table Falls

some land from him—870–446–2218, www.BuffaloRiverRealty.com. While the view from on top of the bluff is stunning, you need to be below the bluffs in order to see the waterfalls. The hike down below is extremely rough and rugged.

The parking spot is right on Hwy. 16. From Nail (between Fallsville and Deer), go 1.2 miles east on Hwy. 16 and PARK on the right side of the road where a driveway takes off down the hill and back to the right. You need to park here even if the gate is open.

Hike down the driveway and follow it through level woods, then down a steep hill to the top of the bluff at .7. TURN LEFT and go another 100 yards or so—there is an easy way down through the bluff there on your right. Once at the base of the bluff TURN RIGHT and follow along the base of the bluff. Just past the first little grotto the bluff will split—take the upper level right in front of you and you will come to the main Tea Table Falls (photo above). You cannot continue past this point and will have to GO BACK to the end of the split in the bluff. GO DOWN to the lower level of the bluff and follow along the base of that bluff. This will take you around past the Lower Tea Table Falls at 1.0 (photo on next page). You can see both falls from that point, and are on forest service land.

CONTINUE along the base of the bluff until you get to the next big falls, Latin Pouroff at 1.3 (photo on next page)—back on private land. It's named for a Latin inscription on a stone that is back under an overhang a little ways past the falls. CONTINUE along the base of the bluff still further until you come to Home Valley Falls at 1.7 (turn page for photo).

Once you have returned to the spot where you came down through the bluff, CONTINUE PAST that spot and follow the base of the bluff to the east until you come to French Falls (turn page for photo), about a quarter mile around the bluff. *Thanks* Edd!

Emergency contact: Newton County Sheriff, 870–446–5124

Lower Tea Table Falls
(the upper falls is in the
background)

Latin Pouroff

Home Valley Falls

Edd French Falls

The Glory Hole – ★★★★★ – 31′

2.0 miles roundtrip, medium hike, GPS not required

Lat/Lon–35 49.326 N, 93 23.611 W • UTM–4 **64** 469 E, 39 **64** 080 N, Fallsville Quad

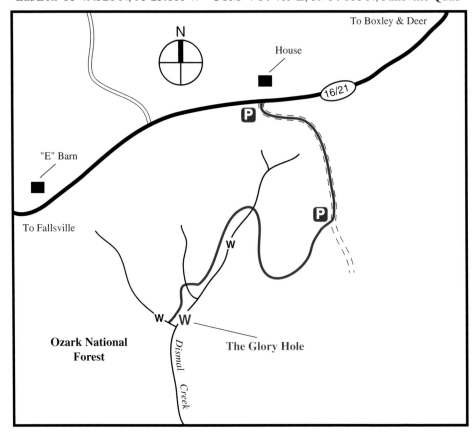

THE GLORY HOLE. This is perhaps the most interesting waterfall of them all. The creek has drilled a large hole right down through the roof of an overhanging bluff, and the resulting waterfall pours out below. The height is measured from the very top of the falls, and includes the thickness of the bluff. It's about a mile hike each way.

To get to the spot to begin this hike, take Hwy. 16/21 east out of Fallsville for 5.7 miles. Here you will pass a red barn on the left that has a large, white "E" on the side of it. Go .5 miles past this barn, and pull off opposite a house that is up on the hill to the left. Park here on the shoulder—there isn't much room. (If you come to the Cassville Baptist Church, you've gone .7 of a mile too far. This pull–off is also 2.3 miles west of Edwards Junction.) If you have a 4wd you can drive down this jeep road another .25 mile and park.

From the highway hike along the jeep road about .25 mile, then TURN RIGHT at the bulletin board onto a lessor roadbed/trail that heads on down the hill. It gets a bit steep as it curves back to the right, and crosses the main stream at the bottom. Stay on this roadbed as it curves back to the left and heads down the hill, eventually turning into plain trail before landing on top of the bluffline. (There is a small waterfall or two upstream.) Be *extremely careful* if you make your way to the bottom!

Emergency contact: Newton County Sheriff, 870–446–5124

The Glory Hole
(from above)

The Glory Hole
(from below)

Lichen Falls – ★★★★ – 28'

.5 mile roundtrip, easy hike, GPS not needed

Lat/Lon–35 45.406 N, 93 31.877 W • UTM–4 **51** 985 E, 39 **56** 891 N, Boston Quad

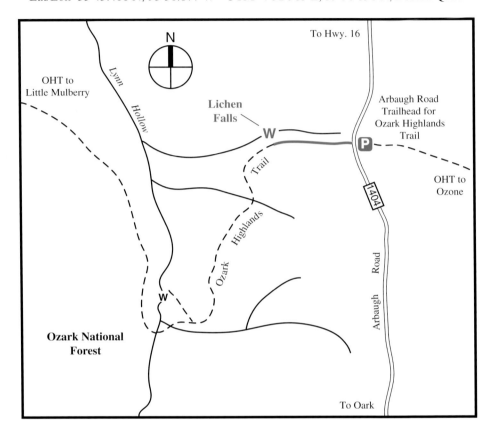

LICHEN FALLS. This is a pretty little double-decked cascade located right next to the Ozark Highlands Trail. It's only a .25 mile hike from the trailhead over level terrain, so most anyone will be able to visit it.

To get to the trailhead, from Fallsville take Hwy. 16 west 2.6 miles and TURN LEFT onto FR#1404/Arbaugh Road (gravel, may not be marked). OR take Hwy. 16 east from Red Star 7.9 miles and TURN RIGHT onto Arbaugh Road. Stay on this road 3.2 miles (bear right at the fork) until you come to the trailhead on the LEFT—it is marked quite well. This road continues on to the community of Oark.

Take the trail across the road to the west. It is level trail and follows a small stream on your right—this is the stream that forms the waterfall. Soon the trail begins to head down the hill just a little bit, and the stream begins to tumble over lichen-covered rocks. The waterfall is located just a little way farther down the stream. If you leave the trail to get a closer look be careful because the hillside is very steep!

If you continued on down the trail past the falls, you would come to a really neat area known as Lynn Hollow (.8 from the trailhead). There is a spur trail to the right that goes to an emerald pool at the base of a series of small waterfalls. Very nice!

Emergency contact: Johnson County Sheriff, 479–754–2200

Lichen Falls

Kings River Falls – ★★★★★ – 10′
1.2 miles roundtrip, easy hike, GPS not needed
Lat/Lon–35 54.114 N, 93 34.466 W • UTM–4 **48** 178 E, 39 **73** 011 N, Weathers Quad

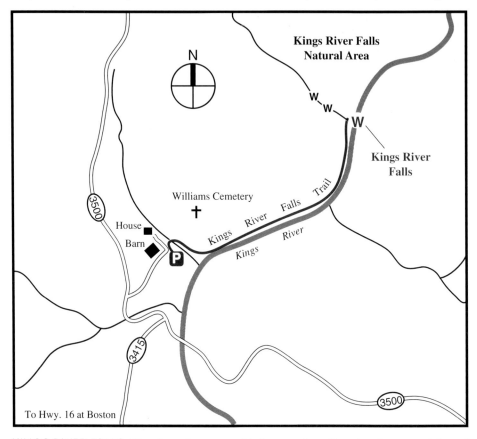

KINGS RIVER FALLS. Year in and year out this is one of my favorite places to visit, and the waterfall there makes it extra special. The trail is easy, even for kids, and the pool below the falls is a good swimming hole in the summertime. Spring brings out many wildflowers along the trail, plus there are lots of wild azaleas and dogwoods blooming. Even though the area is small, there are many places to see and explore. The beginning of this trail is on private property, so be sure to behave yourself.

To get to the trailhead you need to locate the old community of Boston—it is located on Hwy. 16 between Pettigrew and Red Star, and is actually the place where the mighty White River begins. From Boston head north on CR#3175 (gravel) for 2.0 miles and TURN RIGHT at the fork onto CR#3415. Stay on this road 2.3 miles until you come to a "T" intersection—TURN LEFT onto CR#3500 and go across a small creek then TURN RIGHT just past the creek onto what looks like a driveway. Follow this little road until you come to the parking area, which is just before the road ends at a farmhouse. There is not much room to park but it is OK to park wherever you can find the room, even in front of the crumbling barn.

Step across a little creek and TURN RIGHT to begin the hiking trail, which is well used and easy to follow. It goes over to the Kings River and follows it downstream to the

Kings River Falls

left, partially on an old pioneer road. There are many things to see along the way, including an old rock wall next to the trail. Those stones were cleared from the nearby fields and stacked up there more than 100 years ago, and have survived many floods that filled the valley way up over your head.

At .5 you will pass a sign for the Natural Area, and soon after come to the waterfall itself. There once stood a grist mill at the falls that utilized the force of the water to turn millstones that had been brought over from France (the mill had a fireplace and chimney and thus was known as the Chimney Mill). The mill was washed out by a flood in 1914.

There are several waterfalls up the drainage that comes in just above the falls too, and are well worth exploring. The tallest one is on private property, so view it from below.

Emergency contact: Madison County Sheriff, 479–738–2320

Sweden Creek Falls – ★★★★★ – 81'

1.8 miles roundtrip, medium hike/bushwhack, GPS helpful

Lat/Lon–35 58.287 N, 93 27.549 W • UTM–4 **58** 618 E, 39 **80** 670 N, Boxley Quad

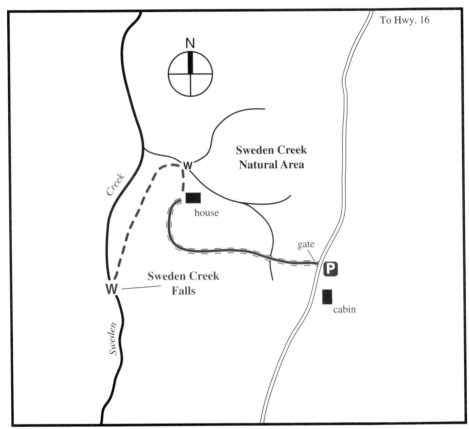

SWEDEN CREEK FALLS. This well-hidden natural area has been surrounded by private property until just recently. Now there is public access to it, and here you will find a remarkable scenic area with towering bluffs, wildflowers, ferns, and a thundering water-fall as its focal point. The first half of the hike is down the road to an old house, but from there it is a bushwhack along the base of the big bluffs where the footing is often tricky.

The turnoff to get to the Natural Area is located on Hwy. 21 between Boxley and Kingston—from Kingston go 5.2 miles south on Hwy. 21 and TURN RIGHT onto the gravel road, or from Boxley go 3.9 miles north on Hwy. 21 and TURN LEFT onto the gravel road. This turnoff is just opposite the turn for Elkhorn Church. Stay on the gravel road for 3.1 miles, then find a place to park. The road down to the old home place is on the right, and will probably be gated.

Hike down the road .4 miles to the old home place (look for some beautiful dogwood trees above the old house if you are there in April). You will come to a garage first—TURN LEFT there and head off into the woods below the house. There is a waterfall about 150 yards or so down there, and just to the left of it is a narrow corridor where you can get down through the bluffline. Once you get to the bottom of the bluff TURN LEFT and follow along the base of the bluff the best you can, or somewhere down below the bluff

Sweden Creek Falls

between it and the creek. This bluff will curve back to the left and forms the eastern wall of the canyon. It will lead you right to the big waterfall at .9. It is one incredible place to say the least, and no wonder the state of Arkansas has protected it as one of its Natural Areas. (There are dozens of "Natural Areas" all over the state—go to the Arkansas Natural Heritage Commission's web site for a complete listing—there is a link to it at www.HikeArkansas.com.) Like all really tall waterfalls in the Ozarks, it looks best when the water levels are high, but it does run most of the wet season.

An alternate way back out to the main road is once you get back to the smaller waterfall and get back up on top of the bluff, simply follow the creek there upstream and you will eventually come out at the road.

Emergency contact: Madison County Sheriff, 479–738–2320

Eagle's Nest Falls – ★★★★ – 41′

.5 mile roundtrip, easy hike/bushwhack, GPS helpful

Lat/Lon–36 13.442 N, 93 39.205 W • UTM–4 **41** 292 E, 40 **08** 786 N, Forum Quad

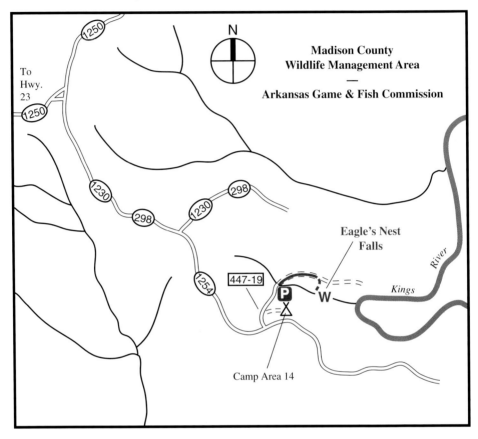

EAGLE'S NEST FALLS. The biggest challenge for this waterfall is simply getting to the parking area—the roads in this wildlife management area have multiple numbers. The waterfall itself pours off into a narrow grotto that is not too far from the Kings River. You can drive pretty close to it and then it's just a short bushwhack down the hill to the top of the falls. Be sure to visit the other great waterfall nearby, Tea Kettle Falls.

The Madison County Wildlife Management Area is located between Huntsville and Eureka Springs, to the east of Hwy. 23. To get to the turnoff, go north out of Huntsville on Hwy. 23 to Forum. Go 3.5 miles and TURN RIGHT onto CR#1235 (gravel) at the Management Area sign. Go another .2 mile where you will meet with CR#1250 at the Management Area headquarters trailer—zero there. **OR** from Eureka Springs, head south on Hwy. 23 for 4.2 miles past the Hwy. 12 intersection and TURN LEFT onto CR#1250 (gravel) at the Management Area Sign. Go .1 mile to the headquarters trailer—zero there. From that intersection go 3.1 miles and TURN RIGHT onto CR#1230/298. Go 1.0 miles and CONTINUE STRAIGHT onto CR#1254–Private Road (CR#1230 turns to the left there). Go another .7 miles and TURN LEFT onto management area road #447–19. Continue down the hill—past Camp Area #14 which is on the right—for .3 and PARK on the right. You should be able to make all of this with a regular vehicle, although that last little bit past the camp area is

Eagle's Nest Falls

questionable with a low-clearance car. If you have a serious 4wd you might be able to go past the parking spot—there is a really bad mud hole that tends to swallow up vehicles.

From the parking area hike on the jeep road past the mud hole and across a small stream—this is the stream that forms the waterfall downstream. The jeep road curves to the right and remains level—stay on it a couple of hundred yards (across a tiny stream) until you come to an open area on the left just after you cross a third small stream (neat area up in the woods to the left). TURN RIGHT and bushwhack down into the woods a couple hundred feet to the creek—you should be at or near the top of the falls. (If you continued along the jeep road it would take you to an overlook of the Kings River.)

Emergency contact: Madison County Sheriff, 479–738–2320

Tea Kettle Falls – ★★★★★ – 46′

2.4 miles roundtrip, easy bushwhack, GPS helpful

Lat/Lon–36 15.980 N, 93 42.892 W • UTM–4 **35** 802 E, 40 **13** 516 N, Rockhouse Quad

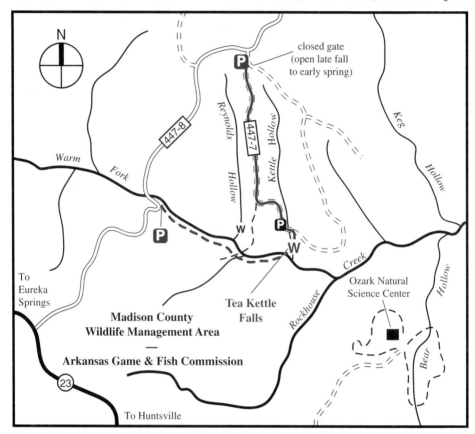

TEA KETTLE FALLS. This is one of the most unique waterfalls in Arkansas. The water has not only drilled a hole down into the top of an overhanging bluff, but before it got all the way through, the water turned 90 degrees and bored a horizontal hole out the front of the bluff! The water actually drops down into a small cave and then exits the bluff. It takes a good bit of water to get this one rolling. There are a couple of different ways to get to this falls—one being an easy and mostly level hike along the stream. At certain times of the year you can also drive very close to the top of the falls with a 4wd vehicle—but the last mile of the road is closed much of the year, and normally open only from the fall through springtime. They close the roads to help protect nesting turkeys.

To get to the turnoff, go north out of Huntsville on Hwy. 23 to Forum, then 6.5 miles and TURN RIGHT onto management area road #447–8 (gravel, and may not be marked, but there is a management area sign on the left just after you turn onto the road). OR from Eureka Springs, head south on Hwy. 23, go 1.4 miles past the Hwy. 12 intersection and TURN LEFT onto management area road #447–8. Go 1.4 miles from the highway and PARK somewhere in the field on the right just before you cross Warm Fork Creek.

From the parking area go across the field to the creek and head downstream. There is an old road that follows the creek but it gets pretty grown up and you may not be able to

Tea Kettle Falls (during high water)

follow it. If you stay on the road or follow the creek you will have to cross the creek either way, so plan to get your feet wet! At about the one mile point you will pass Reynolds Hollow coming in from the left—nice little waterfall there—and there will be lots of interesting bluffs along the way from that point on. Once you get to the next stream that comes in from the left at 1.2, you should be able to hear and/or see the falls—TURN LEFT and follow the stream 100 yards to the base of the falls.

To get to the second parking area, CONTINUE past Warm Fork Creek on the road another 1.3 miles, go up the hill and TURN RIGHT onto management area road #447–7. Either PARK here (if the gate is closed) and hike, or drive down the jeep road (if the gate is open and you have a 4wd). It will take you down the hill to Kettle Hollow Creek, then you leave the road and TURN RIGHT and follow the creek to the top of the falls.

The Ozark Natural Science Center is located about a mile away—up and over the ridge. They have terrific outdoor educational facilities and programs for kids of all ages.

Emergency: Madison County Sheriff, 479–738–2320; Game & Fish, 479–789–5262

Murray Falls – ★★★★★ – 37′

1.0 mile roundtrip, medium bushwhack, GPS helpful
Lat/Lon–35 44.597 N, 93 48.464 W • UTM–4 **26** 980 E, 39 **55** 567 N, Cass Quad

Senyard Falls – ★★★★+ – 29′

Same spot as above, medium bushwhack, GPS helpful
GPS Coordinates are the same as Murray Falls above

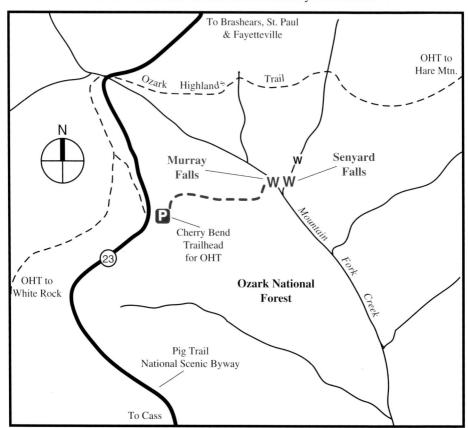

MURRAY FALLS/SENYARD FALLS. When the water is high I highly recommend the short bushwhack down to these waterfalls—most folks go screaming by on the highway above and never know what is below. Dick Murray was a pioneer in the hiking arena in Arkansas long before it became popular, and this falls bears his name. The other falls is named after Roy Senyard, who has worked tirelessly for many years as volunteer maintenance coordinator for the Ozark Highlands Trail, and maintains the popular stretch of the OHT just above these falls. Some folks continue bushwhacking downstream from these falls to get to the Mountain Fork Falls area a couple of miles downstream, but it is a tough trip.

The Cherry Bend Trailhead is located between Cass and Brashears on the Pig Trail National Scenic Byway (Hwy. 23)—take exit 35 off I-40 and head north on Hwy. 23 about 5 miles past Cass, or head east on Hwy. 16 out of Fayetteville, then turn south on Hwy. 23 at Brashears for 5.5 miles.

To get to the falls, head off on a trail behind the bulletin board (the blue-blazed spur

Dick Murray Falls (during high water)

trail that connects to the OHT begins across the highway). It will go to the edge of a steep dropoff and lead you part way down the slope, then end. You want to CONTINUE downhill and generally follow the stream on your left until you come to Murray Falls less than .5 mile downstream (it may be easier to hike up above the creek a ways). If you can get across the creek, it is possible to make your way around to Senyard Falls, which comes in from the left just downstream (turn page for photos). There is a wonderful cascade up above Senyard Falls. Spend some time in this area and rest up for the *steep* climb back out!

Emergency contact: Franklin County Sheriff, 479–667–4127

Cascade above Roy Senyard Falls (during high water)

Roy Senyard Falls (during high water)
Murray Falls is visible in the background.

Spirit Mountain Falls – ★★★+ – 15′

3.0 miles roundtrip (all 3 falls), difficult bushwhack, GPS helpful
Lat/Lon–35 43.248 N, 93 47.419 W • UTM–4 **28** 535 E, 39 **53** 060 N, Cass Quad

Mountain Fork Creek Falls – ★★★+ – 13′

Same trip as above, difficult bushwhack, GPS helpful
Lat/Lon–35 43.406 N, 93 47.517 W • UTM–4 **28** 389 E, 39 **53** 354 N, Cass Quad

Sixty Foot Falls – ★★★★+ – 56′

Same trip as above, difficult bushwhack, GPS helpful
Lat/Lon–35 43.272 N, 93 47.189 W • UTM–4 **28** 883 E, 39 **53** 103 N, Cass Quad

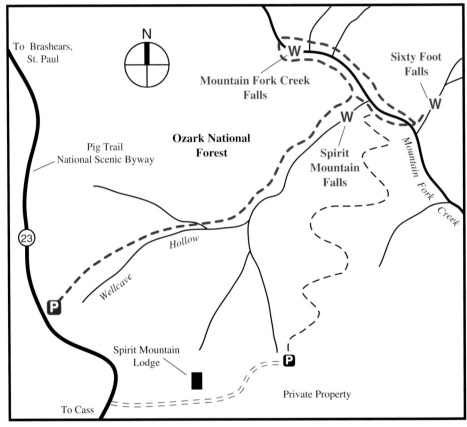

SPIRIT MTN. FALLS/MTN. FORK CREEK FALLS/SIXTY FOOT FALLS. There is a concentration of waterfalls in this one area along Mountain Fork Creek—some nice ones up in the headwaters too (Murray & Senyard Falls). The bushwhack down into the falls is not all that tough, but the nearly 700 foot climb back *up* is. If you want to stay in the area at least one night I recommend using Spirit Mountain Lodge as a base camp—not only will you have a wonderful stay there, but you will have access to a four-wheeler trail that will make the hike a lot easier. Contact them for details at www.spiritmountainlodge.com, or call 479–667–1919.

Take Hwy. 23 north out of Cass, go 2.6 miles past the Hwy. 215 intersection and

Spirit Mountain Falls (above), **Mountain Fork Creek Falls** (below)

Cascade above Sixty Foot Falls

PARK on the right at the big pulloff area that is just across the highway from Whiting Mountain Road (about .2 past the turnoff for Spirit Mtn. Lodge). OR head south on Hwy. 23 from the Cherry Bend Trailhead 2.4 miles to the parking area on the LEFT. There is no specific route to get to these falls—there are many four-wheeler and mountain bike trails in the area on the other side of the creek that you could use for possible access (they are not marked on the map)—but here is a general discussion of the way that I hike into them.

From the parking area head downhill into the woods (east) and just keep going. Down, down, down, any way that you can. There will be a creek on your right and one on your left that will eventually come together—just keep on following them downstream through Wellcave Hollow. You will eventually come to Spirit Mountain Falls at about 1.0. It's not a giant falls, but empties into an emerald pool that is beautiful.

To get to Mountain Fork Creek Falls continue on downstream and you will come to a jeep road just before you hit Mountain Fork Creek (the four-wheeler trail from the Lodge comes in off to your right here)—TURN LEFT and follow the jeep road about .25 mile to Mountain Fork Creek Falls. It's a perfect spot for a dip in the pool!

Sixty Foot Falls

To get to Sixty Foot Falls cross Mountain Fork Creek above the falls, TURN RIGHT and follow the creek back downstream—there is a jeep road you can follow part way. Continue for .4 (across a couple of small streams that may have little waterfalls of their own) until you come to a stream and you should hear the falls up on your left—follow the stream up to the base of the falls. The locals' guess at the height of this falls was pretty close ("Sixty" Foot Falls). If you can make your way up through the bluffline there is a really nice cascade above the falls, and a cave to explore.

To return to the parking area follow the stream below the falls down to Mountain Fork Creek, get across the creek and go upstream to Wellcave Hollow and make the 700 foot climb back out the same way you came in.

Emergency contact: Franklin County Sheriff, 479–667–4127

Spy Rock Falls – ★★★ – 19′

1.0 mile roundtrip, easy hike, GPS not needed

Lat/Lon–35 41.624 N, 93 45.414 W • UTM–4 **31** 534 E, 39 **50** 035 N, Cass Quad

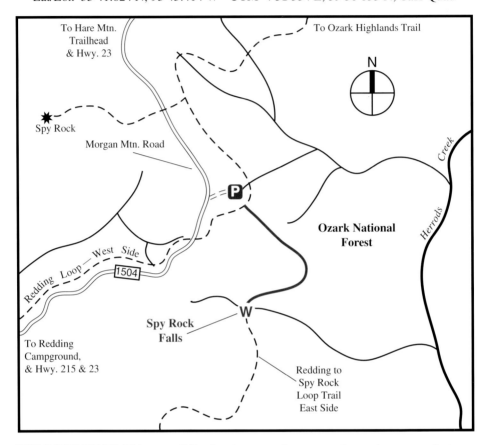

SPY ROCK FALLS. This waterfall takes its name from a nearby rock outcrop that was supposedly used as a lookout point while the Spanish hid hordes of gold nearby. No one has ever found the gold that we know of, but the legend lives on. The falls is located on a loop trail that comes up from Redding Campground, goes out to Spy Rock, and also connects with the Ozark Highlands Trail. We are going to take the easy way in and park near the falls, but you can also hike the 8.8 mile loop trail and make a day of it.

To get to the parking area from Cass, go north on Hwy. 23 and TURN RIGHT onto Hwy. 215 (just as you begin to climb the hill) and follow it about three miles to just past the turnoff to Redding Campground. TURN LEFT onto Morgan Mountain Road/FR#1504 (gravel), then go 1.8 miles up the hill and TURN RIGHT into an open area that is used for camping (there is a small pond nearby).

Head off to the right into the woods along a jeep road where you will find a hiking trail intersection just a couple hundred feet or so ahead. The trail to the right is the West Loop and goes down to Redding Campground, the one on the left goes out to Spy Rock and the OHT—go STRAIGHT AHEAD at this intersection to head towards the falls (you will be on the East Side Loop Trail that also goes down to Redding Campground).

The trail is mostly level and goes downhill just a little bit along an old road trace,

Spy Rock Falls (during high water)

swings around to the right, and comes to the small creek at .5. This is the creek that forms the waterfall, and you will see it just below the trail on your left. It was really pouring buckets when I took the photo above, and while the falls don't normally run that much, they are often a nice little falls worth a trip to go see.

If you want to hike the entire loop trail, start back down at a trailhead that is located just east of the Redding Campground turnoff, and hike the loop in either direction.

Emergency contact: Franklin County Sheriff, 479–667–4127

High Bank Twins – ★★★★★ – 71′
.5 mile roundtrip, easy bushwhack, GPS not needed
Lat/Lon–35 40.846 N, 93 41.216 W • UTM–4 **37** 855 E, 39 **48** 551 N, Yale Quad

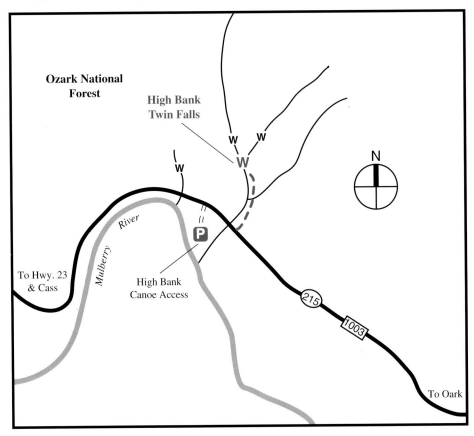

HIGH BANK TWINS. When the water is running high this is one of the most beautiful waterfalls in Arkansas! And it is located right next to a road so the access is quick and easy. You can't really see the falls from the road so few people have been to see it—let's just keep it our little secret.

To get to the High Bank Canoe Access area to park, take Hwy. 23 north from Cass and TURN RIGHT onto Hwy. 215 (just as you begin to climb the hill out of Cass), follow it 9.2 miles and TURN RIGHT into the High Bank Canoe Access parking area which is well signed. This is one of the major put-in points for the popular Mulberry River, a great Ozark floating stream.

From the parking area go out to the road, TURN RIGHT and cross over a stream that is coming in from the left, then leave the road TO THE LEFT and follow that creek upstream (no trail). The woods are level at first, but soon get a little rougher and rocky as you go along. Cross a small stream coming in from the right, and just another hundred yards farther and you will be looking right into the face of these magnificent falls.

Emergency contact: Franklin County Sheriff, 479-667-4127

High Bank Twins (during high water)

Pig Trail Falls – ★★★ – 18′

View from car, no hike involved, GPS not needed

Lat/Lon–35 38.771 N, 93 50.385 W • UTM–4 **23** 994 E, 39 **44** 822 N, Cass Quad

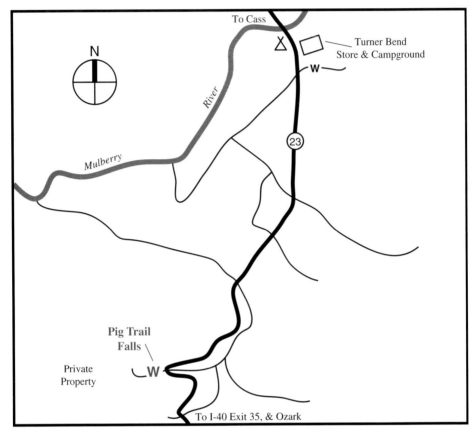

PIG TRAIL FALLS. Many generations of college students from the University of Arkansas going home for the weekend or back to school on Sunday passed by this waterfall. It is located right next to the famous "Pig Trail" highway, which is now a National Scenic Byway. You don't even need to get out of the car to see it!

To get to the falls take exit 35 off I–40 and head north on Hwy. 23. You will pass the falls on the left in a hairpin turn as you are dropping down into the Mulberry River Valley. (The property above the falls is private and not open to explore.) I suggest a lunch stop at the Turner Bend Store, just 1.8 miles north of the waterfall right on the highway—they make great sandwiches (campground and canoe floats too), and there is a nice little waterfall right next to the store that is worth a look when the water is high.

Emergency contact: Franklin County Sheriff, 479–667–4127

Pig Trail Falls (during high water)

Train Trestle Falls – ★★★★ – 31′

2.8 miles roundtrip, medium hike, GPS not needed

Lat/Lon–35 40.655 N, 93 53.139 W • UTM–4 **19** 869 E, 39 **48** 340 N, Bidville Quad

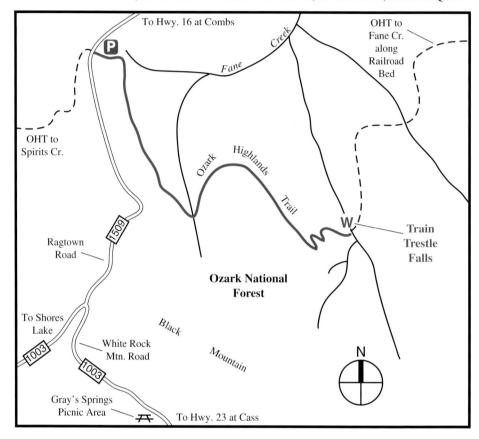

TRAIN TRESTLE FALLS. You can visit a piece of Ozark history at this wonderful water-fall. It is located at the base of what once was a towering wooden trestle where steam locomotives carrying giant white oak logs once roamed. All that remain today are the concrete pilings at the top of the falls, and dozens of rusting iron nuts and bolts that held the mighty timbers together. The Ozark Highlands Trail (OHT) runs along the top of the old railroad bed for several miles and passes this site on the north side of Black Mountain.

Access this area from Cass on Hwy. 23. Go south on Hwy. 23 and turn RIGHT onto White Rock Mountain Road (FR#1003). OR go north from the Turner Bend store on the Mulberry River to get to White Rock Mtn. Rd. This is a rough gravel road, but it is a scenic six-mile drive, and passes through a geological formation known as Bee Rocks (giant honey-combed boulders that are right next to the road—bees nest in them), and then past a unique picnic area called Gray's Spring. The picnic area was built of stone by the Civilian Conser-vation Corps in the 1930's (as were most of the roads in the area, and the cabins and lodge up on White Rock Mountain too). About a half mile past Gray's Spring TURN RIGHT onto Ragtown Road (FR#1509). Go .7 mile and PARK on the right just beyond where the OHT crosses the road. This is the same parking spot as for Spirits Creek/Robinson Falls.

From the road head east on the OHT (blazed white) as it drops down the hill—TURN

Train Trestle Falls (during high water)

RIGHT onto a logging road and follow it for a little ways, then TURN RIGHT again onto another old road trace that will take you uphill slightly, past OHT milepost #26, then TURN LEFT onto pure trail just after the mile marker. The trail swings around the hillside to the left past a beautiful moss-covered cascade, then intersects another log road that will take you through an old clearcut area. TURN LEFT off this road after a while onto regular trail, and drop on down the hill to a larger creek at 1.4—this is the gorge the old trestle spanned, and the waterfall is located just downstream.

Emergency contact: Franklin County Sheriff, 479–667–4127

Spirits Creek Falls – ★★★★ – 8′

2.4 miles roundtrip, medium hike, GPS helpful

Lat/Lon–35 41.227 N, 93 54.482 W • UTM–4 **17** 853 E, 39 **49** 416 N, Bidville Quad

Robinson Falls (2) – ★★★+ – 17′/21′

Add .2 mile to above distance, easy bushwhack from above, GPS helpful

Lat/Lon–35 41.262 N, 93 54.613 W • UTM–4 **17** 656 E, 39 **49** 483 N, Bidville Quad

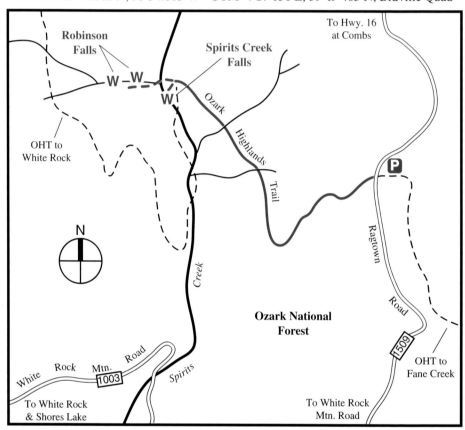

SPIRITS CREEK FALLS. Spirits Creek has long been an oasis along the Ozark Highlands Trail (OHT). The falls are not all that tall, but there is a certain magical feeling about the place—a very happy "spirit" must live there. The first time I ever camped beside this creek everyone in our group woke up around 3 in the morning. After a bit of discussion we realized that the creek had suddenly gone silent— it had frozen solid! The temperature was five below zero. It was a great hike the next morning through a winter wonderland.

Access this area from Cass on Hwy. 23. Go south on 23 (or north from the Turner Bend store on the Mulberry River) and turn RIGHT onto White Rock Mountain Road (FR#1003). This is a rough gravel road, but it is a scenic five or six mile drive, and passes through a geological formation known as Bee Rocks (giant honeycombed boulders that are right next to the road—bees nest in them), and then past a unique one-table picnic area called Gray's Spring. The picnic area was built of stone by the Civilian Conservation Corps in the 1930's (as were most of the roads in the area, and the cabins and lodge up on White Rock Mountain

Spirits Creek Falls

too). About a half mile past Gray's Spring TURN RIGHT onto Ragtown Road (FR#1509), go .7 mile and PARK on the right just beyond where the OHT crosses the road. This is the same parking spot as for Train Trestle Falls, but you hike in the opposite direction.

You can also get here from the other direction: Take the Mulberry exit off I-40 (exit #24) and head north on Hwy. 215 to Fern (past the turnoff to Devils Canyon), continue another three miles on the highway and TURN LEFT onto FR#1505/CR#75 (paved), continue past Shores Lake (pavement ends, road is called Bliss Ridge Road) another four miles up the hill and TURN RIGHT onto White Rock Mtn. Road (FR#1003) and take it down the mountain across Salt Fork Creek, up and over Potato Knob Mountain, down the mountain to Spirits Creek, and then up the hill to Ragtown Road where you will TURN LEFT and go .7 mile and park at the OHT parking spot. Whew, that was a mouthful!

To get to the falls take the OHT (blazed white) west from Ragtown Road. It will drop gradually down into the Spirits Creek drainage. When you get to the very bottom at 1.2 the trail will land on an old logging road and turn abruptly to the left—you want to actually TURN RIGHT here and go the opposite direction on the road trace for just 100 feet or so, then leave the road TO THE LEFT and head down the slope, across a primitive camping area to the creek below. This area is small and fragile, so handle with care.

ROBINSON FALLS. The first time I found this pair of waterfalls I was hiking with Bob and Dawna Robinson on a warm day in April. They had been in charge of organizing volunteers from all over the United States to keep the OHT maintained for many years,

Lower Robinson Falls

and did quite a bit of trail work themselves too. We were on the hillside above Spirits Creek inspecting the trail when the sky got really black, opened up and began to pour buckets. The smart one in our group had rain gear, but Bob and I only had t-shirts and shorts to protect us from the blast. Anyway, we all survived just fine, and found these two beautiful waterfalls in the process. I have named them in honor of the great work these two fine folks did for the trail.

To reach the falls from Spirits Creek, simply go upstream from the waterfall on the creek a short distance, cross the creek where you can, and follow the side stream uphill that comes in from the west—you will get to the base of the lower falls after only 100 yards or so, and will be able to look up and see the upper falls from there.

Emergency contact: Franklin County Sheriff, 479–667–4127

Upper Robinson Falls

White Rock Creek Falls – ★★★★ – 31'

2.6 miles roundtrip, medium hike, GPS helpful

Lat/Lon–35 40.397 N, 93 58.267 W • UTM–4 **12** 131 E, 39 **47** 936 N, Bidville Quad

White Rock Creek Cascade – ★★★+ – 10'

Add .6 mile to above distance, medium hike, GPS not needed

Lat/Lon–35 40.264 N, 93 58.103 W • UTM–4 **12** 376 E, 39 **47** 689 N, Bidville Quad

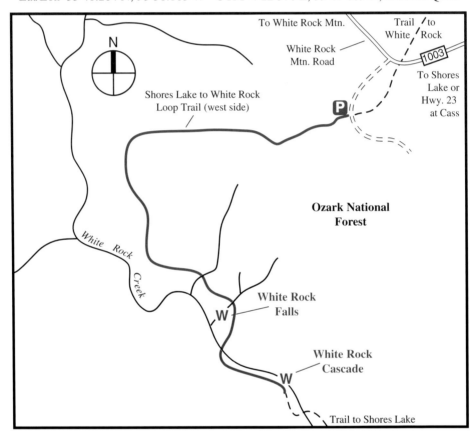

WHITE ROCK CREEK FALLS/CASCADE. My first picture ever published in a national maga-zine was of this waterfall—in the September, 1983 issue of ***Backpacker***. The falls are located along a popular loop trail, and near the best sunset spot in the Ozarks—White Rock Mountain.

Take the Mulberry exit off I-40 (exit #24) and head north on Hwy. 215 to Fern (past the turnoff to Devils Canyon). Continue another three miles on the highway and TURN LEFT onto FR#1505/CR#75 (paved). Go past Shores Lake (pavement ends, road is called Bliss Ridge Road) another four miles up the hill and TURN LEFT onto White Rock Mtn. Road (FR#1003). Go .6 mile and TURN LEFT onto a jeep road, then follow it a couple hundred yards and park where the Shores Lake to White Rock trail crosses it (blazed blue).

From the parking area get on the trail to the RIGHT and head off into the woods. The trail eases up a hill, then begins a *long* descent into the White Rock Creek drainage. It levels out some and curves around a couple of small streams. At 1.3 it crosses a stream that has some cascades above and you can tell that the water goes over a dropoff down be-

White Rock Creek Falls (right)

White Rock Creek Cascade (below)

low—this is the falls. The best way to get to it is to continue on the main trail until it has landed in the flat bottoms, then bushwhack back to your right and up into the little grotto where the waterfall is. To get to the cascade, go back to the trail and continue hiking. Soon you will have to cross White Rock Creek, and then will follow it downstream just a little way further on the trail until you reach the cascade at 1.6. (You can also get to these waterfalls by hiking the Shores Lake to White Rock Loop Trail from Shores Lake—TURN RIGHT into the Shores Lake Campground to get to the trailhead, then take the West Side Loop to the cascade at 2.8, and on to the falls at 3.1.)

Emergency contact: Franklin County Sheriff, 479-667-4127

Rattlesnake Falls – ★★★★ – 29′

.25 mile roundtrip, easy bushwhack, GPS not needed

Lat/Lon–35 41.604 N, 94 01.726 W • UTM–4 **06** 935 E, 39 **50** 220 N, Fern Quad

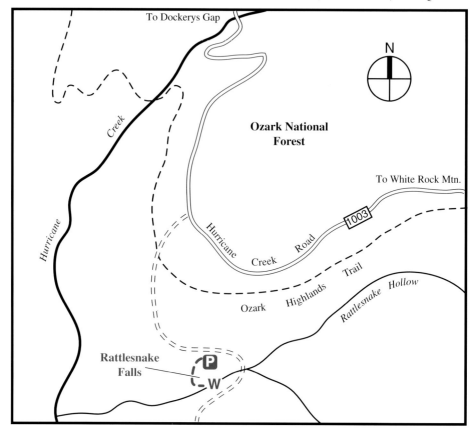

RATTLESNAKE FALLS. Here is a nice little out-of-the-way waterfall that is easy to get to and few people have visited. It's a short, easy bushwhack to get to it, and not too far off the Ozark Highlands Trail. I found out about this falls when friend Bill Herring e-mailed me a photo of him going over it in a kayak!

OK, try to follow these directions: Take the Mulberry exit off of I-40 (exit #24) and head north on Hwy. 215 to Fern (past the turnoff to Devils Canyon). Continue another three miles on the highway and TURN LEFT onto FR#1505/CR#75 (paved). Continue past Shores Lake (pavement ends, road is called Bliss Ridge Road) another four miles up the hill and TURN LEFT onto White Rock Mtn. Road (FR#1003). Follow it 2.2 miles and TURN LEFT onto Hurricane Creek Road (turn right to go to White Rock Mtn.). Go 4.7 miles and TURN LEFT onto an unmarked dirt road, and finally go .7 mile and PARK on the right just before you cross the creek. From Mountainburg—see directions to Dockery Gap Falls—then continue on past Hurricane Creek .7 mile up the hill, then TURN RIGHT on the unmarked dirt road, go .7 mile and PARK on the right.

From the parking area you can either continue along the road until you get to the creek, then follow it downstream to the top of the falls (very slick there!), or simply head out into the woods to the south until you come to the stream and waterfall—it's not very

Rattlesnake Falls (during high water)

far to the falls. If you hike downstream a ways there is access down through the bluffline and then you can come back upstream to the base of the falls. If you get down to the base, gaze on up to the top of the falls and just imagine a guy going over that in a *kayak!*

Emergency contact: Crawford County Sheriff, 479-474-2261

Dockery Gap Falls – ★★★★★ – 36′

3.0 miles roundtrip, difficult bushwhack, GPS recommended

Lat/Lon–35 43.231 N, 94 01.030 W • UTM–4 **08** 017 E, 39 **53** 218 N, Fern Quad

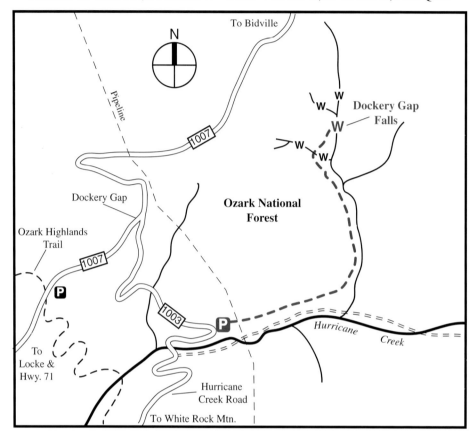

DOCKERY GAP FALLS. If you come to this spot during really high water, you will see more waterfalls than you can count! This grotto is tucked away back up in a side canyon of Hurricane Creek, and it takes a good bit of bushwhacking to reach it (no trail). Be sure to visit the nearby Rattlesnake Falls while you are in the area.

From Mountainburg, take Hwy. 71 south 2.6 miles to the top of the hill. TURN LEFT onto CR#348 (paved). Go 14.1 miles to Dockery Gap (the road will turn to dirt and to FR#1007 near Locke) and TURN RIGHT onto FR#1003 (Hurricane Creek Rd.). Then go .9 mile down the hill and PARK on the left side of the road at a hairpin curve (about .25 mile before you cross Hurricane Creek). You will be able to look over the edge and see Hurricane Creek below. You can also get to this spot from the White Rock Mountain area—just take FR#1003 (Hurricane Creek Rd.) to the west 5.4 miles to the bridge across Hurricane Creek, then continue on to the second sharp curve and PARK on the right.

Leave the road and head across the hillside along a bench. You'll soon cross a pipeline right of way, then back into the woods again. Stay on the level as best you can, just bushwhacking generally straight ahead. When you begin to come to a large drainage in front of you, follow the contour of the hillside around to the left, and up into that drainage.

As you work your way up into this drainage you can either stay a bench or two above

Dockery Gap Falls (during high water)

the creek, or simply go down and follow the creek upsteam—there will be some steep and rugged terrain either way. You will eventually come to a waterfall near the creek that enters from a side drainage on your left—there is also a larger one up that same little drainage. Continue on the main creek past these, and you will come to the big falls. It is quite a place when the water is running high! It's about 1.5 miles back to the road—the best way is simply to go back the same way you came in.

Emergency contact: Crawford County Sheriff, 479–474–2261

Devils Canyon Falls – ★★★★★ – 63′

2.0 miles roundtrip, difficult bushwhack, GPS recommended

Lat/Lon–35 38.255 N, 94 02.093 W • UTM–4 **06** 317 E, 39 **44** 036 N, Fern Quad

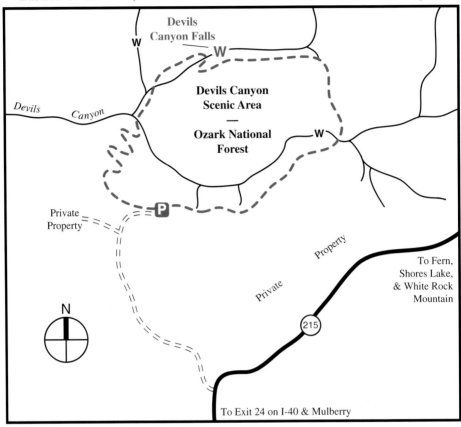

DEVILS CANYON FALLS. This seldom-visited scenic area is quite rugged, but is located right off the highway and is easy to get to—at least to get to the edge of it. Hiking around inside the area is another matter—there are no trails, and the terrain can be brutal. But the rewards are plenty, and the waterfall is really spectacular.

Take the Mulberry/Hwy. 215 exit (#24) off I-40 east of Ft. Smith and head north on Hwy. 215 to the tiny community of Fern. Zero your odometer there and head back south of Fern on Hwy. 215—go 1.4 miles and TURN RIGHT (west) onto an unmarked dirt road. A truck or 4wd vehicle helps as this road gets a little bit rough. Follow the road up and over a small hill—STAY STRAIGHT at the intersection (the left fork goes into private property)—and PARK once you come to the edge of the canyon .6 mile from the highway.

Once again there are no trails, but here is the route I normally take. Continue on the jeep road to the east from the parking spot—you'll be hiking right along the edge of the canyon, which is off to your left. The farther you go the worse this little road gets. Follow it around the edge of the canyon until you drop down a bit and come to a creek (there are some nice cascades downstream). Wade the creek and head up the hill and a little bit to your left, and away from that road trace—hike towards a low spot in the ridge if you can see one (a GPS helps a lot!). Bushwhack up into the "saddle," then continue down the other side, veering to the left as you go. Once you hit the creek TURN LEFT and follow it

Devils Canyon Falls (during high water)

downstream until you come to the top of the falls. It is ***extremely dangerous*** at this point! You might be able to make it down to the base of the falls, but it is pretty tough.

To get back to the parking area, either return the way you came in, or loop around the other side of the hill (it's about a mile either way). To loop back, head downstream from the falls. Once you reach the main stream, find a way across it, then bushwhack *up* the hillside and back to the parking area—it is *very steep!*

Emergency contact: Franklin County Sheriff, 479–667–4127

Artist Point Falls – ★★★★ – 15′

1.2 miles roundtrip, medium hike, GPS not needed

Lat/Lon–35 43.220 N, 94 07.972 W • UTM–3 **97** 552 E, 39 **53** 311 N, Mountainburg Quad

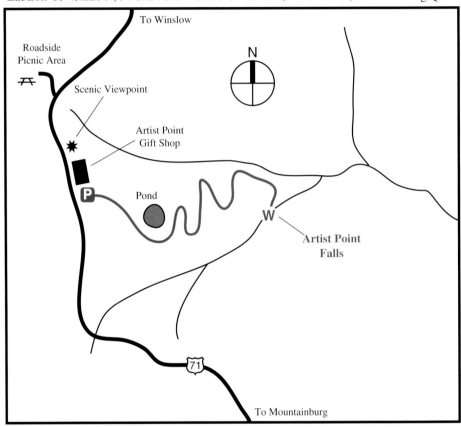

ARTIST POINT FALLS. This is a private trail but the good folks at Artist Point Gift Shop welcome visitors, and even have a place for you to park around the side of the building. Be sure to stop by the gift shop and say hi, and look at the mini-museum inside. The trail is a bit steep getting down to the waterfall area, but if there is lots of water running you will be rewarded with a number of different beautiful cascades. There are also some Indian carvings in the rocks along the way, and a natural bridge of stone. Oh yea, the view from the far end of the gift shop is quite spectacular, looks out over the new Lake Ft. Smith area, and is one of the best sunrise views in the Ozarks.

Artist Point is located about eight miles north of Mountainburg on scenic Hwy. 71.

The trail begins near the back of the gift shop on the right—PARK there. It heads steeply down an old road, through a yard area and pond, then heads into the woods. The trail continues down the hill at a pretty good clip, swinging back and forth, past rock formations and a creek. It eventually curves back to the right, underneath an overhanging rock, then on over to another creek, where the trail ends. There are waterfalls both above and below this point. Spend some time, take a lot of pictures, and rest up for the steep climb out!

Emergency: Crawford County Sheriff, 479–474–2261; Gift Shop, 479–369–2226

**Artist Point
Falls**
(during high water)

Twin Falls at Devil's Den – ★★★★ – 47′/56′

1.5 miles roundtrip, easy hike, GPS not needed

Lat/Lon–35 46.928 N, 94 14.558 W • UTM–3 **87** 709 E, 39 **60** 287 N, Winslow Quad

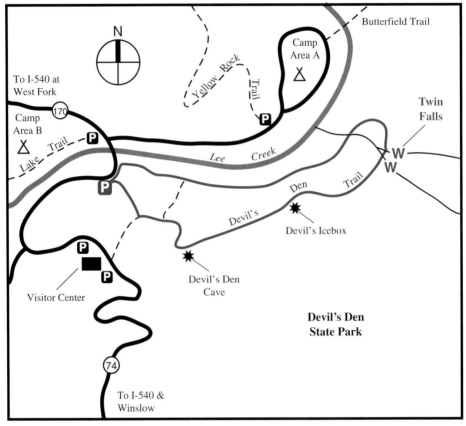

TWIN FALLS AT DEVIL'S DEN. This is one of the most popular hiking trails in the state. Most folks come to explore the little Devil's Den Cave, but I particularly love the waterfall because it is about the only one around I know of that has a bridge crossing the middle of it—reminds me of the giant waterfalls in the Columbia River Gorge in Oregon. You will also want to go see the spillway at the small lake—a beautiful cascade hand crafted by the Civilian Conservation Corps in the 1930's.

Devil's Den State Park is a longtime family favorite destination and has campsites, rental cabins, a swimming pool, picnic area, and many trails including the Butterfield Backpacking Trail, horse and mountain biking trails. To get there from I-540 between Fayetteville and Ft. Smith, either take the Winslow exit (#45) and follow Hwy. 74 to the park, or take the West Fork exit (#53) and follow Hwy. 170 to the park. The trailhead is located on the south side of the bridge that spans Lee Creek.

The trail is well marked, and there are interpretive stops along the way that are keyed to a brochure that you can pick up at the visitor center. From the main parking area the trail heads up the hill just a little bit, then swings around up to Devil's Den Cave (it's a crevice that goes 550 feet back into the hillside—be sure to bring a flashlight). The trail levels out some and passes through lots of broken bluffs and interesting geological formations, past the Devil's Icebox crevice, and finally comes to Twin Falls at about the one mile point.

Twin Falls at Devil's Den
(this is a portion of the left falls of the twin)

The trail actually goes under the first of the two falls, and then crosses the middle of the second one via a wooden bridge (pictured above). From the falls the trail drops down the hill and follows alongside Lee Creek all the way back to the trailhead.

Emergency: Washington County Sheriff, 479–444–1850; Park office 479–761–3325

Natural Dam – ★★★+ – 8' x 187'

No hiking required—view from car, GPS not needed

Lat/Lon–35 38.998 N, 94 23.855 W • UTM–3 **73** 496 E, 39 **45** 816 N, Natural Dam Quad

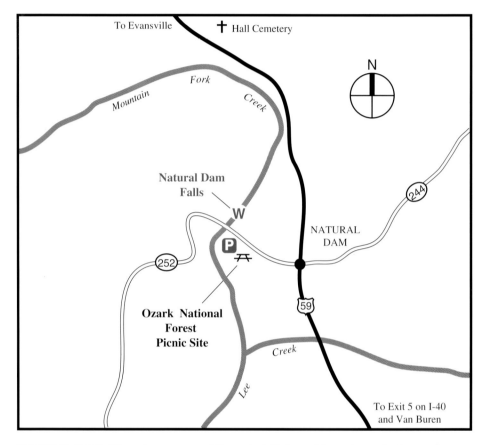

NATURAL DAM. How about a waterfall nearly 200 feet wide, and you don't even have to get out of your car to see it! That's the case with Natural Dam, which is, just like the name suggests, a natural wall of rock that spans the entire width of Mountain Fork Creek, creating a dam of sorts, and a great waterfall. It's a great spot to stop and have a picnic lunch at while on a tour through the Ozarks.

To get to Natural Dam, take Exit #5 on I–40 at Van Buren and head north on Hwy. 59, then TURN LEFT at the community of Natural Dam—the picnic area and falls are within sight of the turn.

Emergency contact: Crawford County Sheriff, 479–474–2261

Natural Dam

Tanyard Creek Falls – ★★★+ – 12′

.8 mile roundtrip, easy hike, GPS not needed

Lat/Lon–36 28.063 N, 94 15.509 W • UTM–3 **87** 263 E, 40 **36** 352 N, Hiwasse Quad

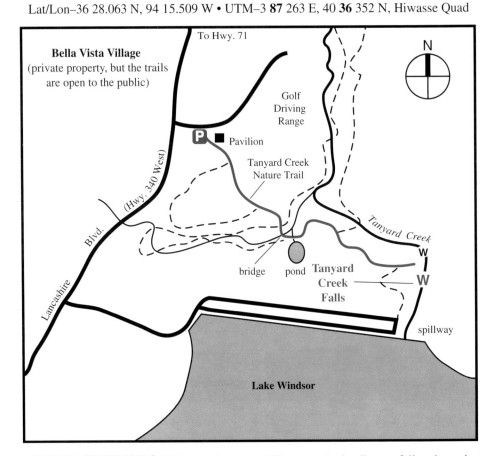

TANYARD CREEK FALLS. This one almost qualifies as an "urban" waterfall, at least that is what I thought when I heard about it and went up to hike to it. But much to my great surprise what I found was not only an interesting little waterfall and cascade, but a first class nature trail, all of that right in the middle of a busy community. It is located within the community of Bella Vista, nestled in between a couple of lakes, a golf course, and a driving range. The waterfall actually comes off the end of the spillway for a man-made lake (even runs in the summertime), but I decided to include it in this book because the nature trail is so very nice, and there really aren't many waterfalls in this extreme north-west part of the state. All of the property around this waterfall and trail is private, and unless you are a Bella Vista property owner you are not welcome (that includes the road on top of the dam that goes very near to the waterfall). But the trail is open to the public.

And what a great trail it is—built and maintained by volunteers, there must be 100 or more interpretive signs all over the place, benches, plus a number of bridges that cross two different creeks. And it is all mostly level so anyone can hike it, even smaller kids. The entire trail system is more than three miles long, but the hike directly to the waterfall is less than a mile roundtrip. Oh yea—and I've never seen anything like this at a trailhead before—but there is a water faucet there with a stainless steel bowl attached that is specifi-

Tanyard Creek Falls

cally for watering your dog— being a dog owner I find that a really nice touch.

To get to the trailhead, head north on Hwy. 71 and take the Hwy. 340/Town Center exit, then TURN LEFT. Go just about a mile on Hwy. 340/Lancashire Blvd. and TURN LEFT —it is signed as "Tanyard Creek Recreation." Then TURN RIGHT into the parking lot. There is an open pavilion there, and restrooms.

The trail begins next to the pavilion—TURN RIGHT and follow the paved trail out across an open field. You will pass two intersections with a paved trail that loops out through the field to the right, but you stay STRAIGHT AHEAD. There is a golf driving range off to your left. At the far end of the field you will pass under a powerline, come to the end of the pavement, then into the woods to a large signboard. GO STRAIGHT AHEAD past this sign to the bridge across the creek (there are trails to the right and to the left at the sign).

TURN LEFT after you cross the bridge and follow the trail past a little pond. The trail curves to the left over near the creek, then back to the right along a line of trees, and comes to an intersection after 100 yards or so—TURN RIGHT (the other trail crosses the stream over to the left and continues on downstream). Head on up the hill and into a beautiful stand of large trees—you can hear and see some cascades over on the creek. CONTINUE STRAIGHT at the next intersection, and you will come to the waterfall overlook at .4.

You can easily hike to this falls and back in 30 minutes, but allow plenty of time to read the little signs, and hike some of the rest of the trail if you can—at the very least hike the trail that is to the left of the pond on your way back—very nice indeed!

Emergency contact: Benton County Sheriff, 501–271–1008

Arkansas River Valley Waterfalls

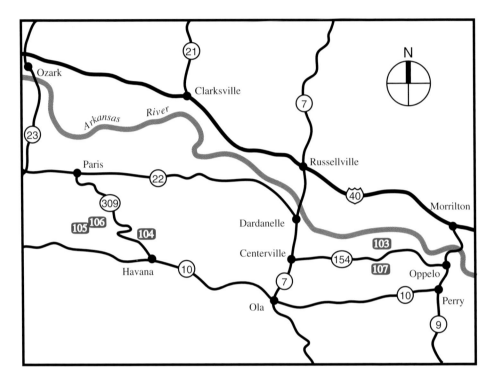

You don't expect to find waterfalls *down in the valley,* and you seldom ever do. In Arkansas there is a line of mountains that rise up from the floor of the Arkansas River Valley and are not a part of either the Ouachita or Ozark mountain ranges. They are anything but valley mountains, and in fact one of them is the tallest mountain in Arkansas—Mt. Magazine. The combination of moisture from the big river below and the relatively high elevations produce a lot of rain, which pours off of the mountains as waterfalls. I've selected some of the best here, including one of the most magnificent waterfalls in the state, Cedar Falls. Each of these waterfalls is located in a rather scenic park to begin with, so your trips to go visit them will be especially rewarding.

Fall #	Name	Beauty Rating	Height	Hike Difficulty	Page #
103	Cedar Falls	★★★★★	95	Medium	**194**
104	Hardy Falls	★★★	8	Easy	**190**
105	Mt. Magazine Cascade	★★★★	100+	Easy	**192**
106	Mt. Magazine Falls	★★★★	28	Medium	**192**
107	Seven Hollows Grotto	★★★★	18	Medium	**196**

Hardy Falls – ★★★ – 8′

Short hike or view from your car, GPS not needed

Lat/Lon–35 09.107 N, 93 33.792 W • UTM–4 **48** 717 E, 38 **89** 812 N, Magazine Mtn. NE Quad

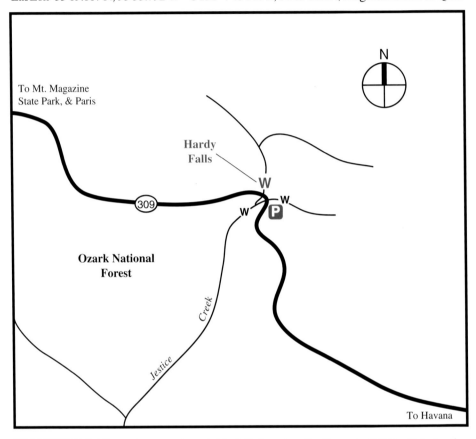

HARDY FALLS. The main attraction of this falls is not really the waterfall itself, but rather the unique rock work right in front of it. When the difficult job of designing a road up to the top of the highest mountain in Arkansas was being considered back in the 1930's, they brought in an expert named James W. Hardy. His craftsmanship in stone remains today in the form of culverts that are, well, beautiful. You can see these works of art at Hardy Falls. As you can see from the photo here the culverts line right up with the waterfall, showing both off to their fullest. While I don't recommend standing in one of the culverts during periods of high water, most of the time you can climb down into them and get this great view. Besides the waterfall at the upper end of the culverts, there are also some nice cascades down below, although they require a bit of a scramble to reach.

To get to Hardy Falls from Paris, take Hwy. 309 south about 17 miles to the state park visitor center located right on the highway. Continue on Hwy. 309 another 6.0 miles from there and you will find the falls just off to the left in a sharp curve—PARK just beyond on the left side of the road. You can also get to the falls by going north on Hwy. 309 from Havana.

While you are up this high, be sure to go hike the short Signal Hill Trail at Mt. Magazine State Park up to the highest point in Arkansas (2,753 feet), visit the other two water-

James W. Hardy Falls
(photo was taken in the moonlight)

falls at the park (descriptions follow), and stop by the visitor center for the complete story of Mt. Magazine with some really nice exhibits and programs.

Emergency: Logan County Sheriff, 479–963–3271; Visitor Center, 479–963–8502

Mt. Magazine Cascade – ★★★★ – 100+′

1.0 mile roundtrip, easy hike, GPS not needed

Lat/Lon–35 10.311 N, 93 39.340 W • UTM–4 **40** 310 E, 38 **92** 089 N, Magazine Mtn. NE Quad

Mt. Magazine Falls – ★★★★ – 28′

.7 mile roundtrip, easy/medium bushwhack, GPS not needed

Lat/Lon–35 10.148 N, 93 38.257 W • UTM–4 **41** 952 E, 38 **91** 777 N, Magazine Mtn. NE Quad

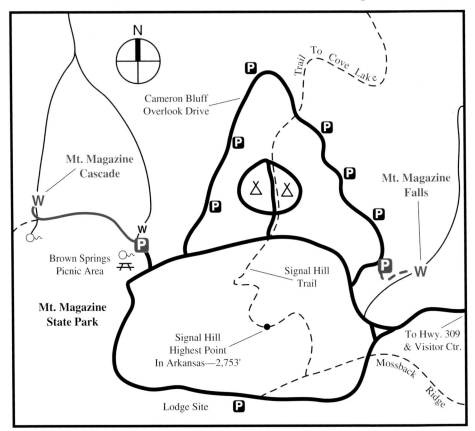

MT. MAGAZINE CASCADE/FALLS. How in the world did waterfalls get all the way up here? Sure enough, there are a couple of surprisingly scenic waterfalls within spitting distance of the tallest point in Arkansas.

To get to Mt. Magazine State Park, take Hwy. 309 south out of Paris 17 miles to the visitor center—TURN RIGHT there and drive to the far end of the park and PARK at the Brown Springs Picnic Area. (Look for rare Maple Leaf Oak trees.) Take the level trail out the back of the picnic area and follow it until you come to a creek about .5 mile in—the **Cascade** is just down to the right, and the waters tumble out of sight and far down the mountain. To get to the **Falls** go back and drive around the Cameron Bluff Overlook Drive and PARK at the very last pulloff (it is a one-way road). There is no real trail—you simply head down the steep hillside to the right into the woods, under a bluff known as Barn Cave, until you come to the creek, then simply follow it downstream 100 yards to the falls.

Emergency: Logan County Sheriff, 479–963–3271; Visitor Center, 479–963–8502

Mt. Magazine Cascade
(right)

Mt. Magazine Falls
(below)

Cedar Falls – ★★★★★ – 95′

2.0 miles roundtrip, medium hike, GPS not needed
Lat/Lon–35 07.289 N, 92 56.046 W • UTM–5 **06** 019 E, 38 **86** 309 N, Adona Quad

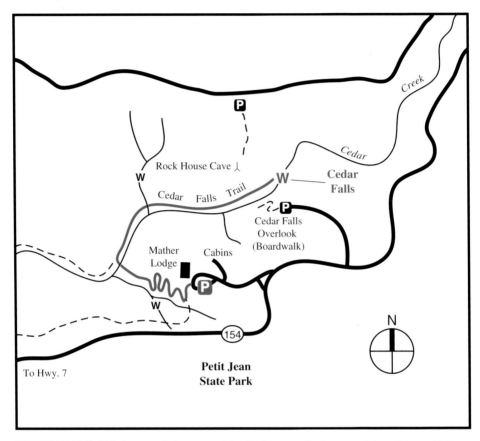

CEDAR FALLS. This is one of the most visited, photographed, powerful, and beautiful waterfalls in Arkansas. You will remember it for a long time. There are two ways to view this falls–via a wheelchair-accessible boardwalk from above, or by taking the Cedar Falls Trail down to the base of the falls. The hike back up from the base is a steep one, although I see tons of kids and folks of all ages making the trek all the time. Be sure to bring along plenty of water and allow some extra time for the hike out. We did not measure this falls, and were told by park staff that the height was estimated at 95 feet.

Petit Jean State Park is one of the finest examples of the craftsmanship done by the Civilian Conservation Corps back in the 1930's, and you will see many examples of their stone work throughout the park. To get to Petit Jean from Russellville, take Hwy. 7 south to Centerville, then TURN LEFT onto Hwy. 154 and follow it to the top of the mountain. Or from Morrilton take Hwy. 9 south to Oppelo and TURN RIGHT onto Hwy. 154 and take it up to the mountain. There is a sign for the overlook turnoff, and you will park at Mather Lodge for the Cedar Falls Trail, which begins right at the lodge.

The trail begins its drop down the steep hillside almost immediately, switchbacking back and forth, back and forth (be sure *not* to shortcut any of the switchbacks!). If the water is running well you might see a nice waterfall out to your left as you go down. You

Cedar Falls

will also have some time to look at it on the way back up—while you are standing there resting and about to die from the climb! When the trail finally hits bottom it crosses Cedar Creek on a tall, narrow bridge—TURN RIGHT when you get to the other side. This trail will follow the creek upstream all the way to the falls. You will cross a side creek part way up, and there is a nice waterfall up to your left that can sometimes be seen and heard from the trail. The trail ends at Cedar Falls at the 1.0 mile point (no swimming in the pool). To return to the parking area you have to go back out the same way that you came in—up that nice little hill with all of those switchbacks! Take it slow and easy and enjoy the scenery on the way up. Be sure to visit the Seven Hollows Grotto Falls too (see next page).

Emergency contact: Yell County Sheriff, 479–495–2811; Park Office, 501–727–5441

Seven Hollows Grotto – ★★★★ – 18′

4.5 miles roundtrip, medium hike, GPS not needed

Lat/Lon–35 5.877 N, 92 56.924 W • UTM–5 **4** 688 E, 38 **83** 698 N, Adona Quad

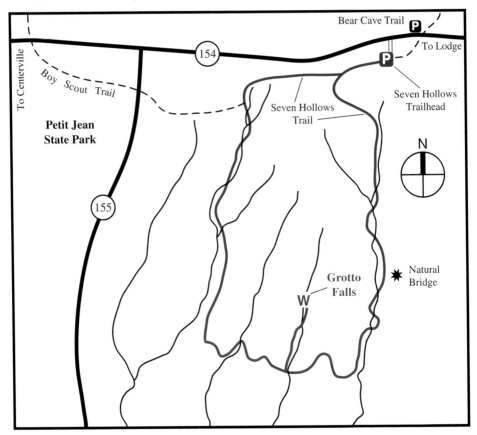

SEVEN HOLLOWS GROTTO. This waterfall is located halfway around the loop of one of the best hiking trails in the state. Each of the many hollows the trail visits is lined with bluffs on both sides, and you are actually winding in and out of canyons of stone. Tucked away in one of the canyons is a "grotto" where the creek spills down over the bluff—a really neat spot! It's not the tallest waterfall around, but is certainly one of the most scenic.

Petit Jean State Park is one of our most popular parks and gets a great deal of traffic, as does this hiking trail. To get to the trailhead at Petit Jean State Park, take Hwy. 7 south out of Russellville to Centerville, turn left onto Hwy. 154 and go 14.1 miles, then turn right into the trailhead parking area soon after you enter the park. From Morrilton, take Hwy. 9 south a few miles to Oppelo and turn right onto Hwy. 154, then turn left into the trailhead at the far end of the park. Everything is signed really well. In fact, there are even mile-point signs every half mile along the trail.

The Seven Hollows area was burned by a major fire in August of 2000, and you will see evidence of this for many years. It is all recovering well, and the new forest is thriving. The trail heads out into the burned area and comes to an intersection right away. The sign says the Grotto is to the right, but I prefer to hike this trail clockwise. Since the waterfall is located about halfway around the loop, it really doesn't matter which way you go, and I

Seven Hollows Grotto

highly recommend that you hike the entire loop. So TURN LEFT at the intersection.

The trail gradually heads downhill and enters the first of many bluff-lined canyons, following a little stream. There are many inviting places to explore. At 1.3 you will find a large natural bridge of stone that is worth some extra time. The trail crosses the creek a few times, then leaves the canyon to the right and climbs out and up on top of a ridgetop, where you will visit a wonderful wildflower-filled glade. Lots of collared lizards running around up there, too. At 2.1 the trail drops down to another creek and to a trail intersection—TURN RIGHT here and follow the spur trail up into the "Grotto" to the falls.

For the rest of your hike simply return to the main trail and continue on. The trail climbs up onto the next little ridgetop—more wildflowers and lizards—then drops back down into another hollow. It works its way back uphill some, then back down into yet another hollow. Here you will begin a gradual rise back up to the trailhead, past many towering bluffs and interesting rock features. It is all quite beautiful! At 3.8 there is an intersection with the Boy Scout Trail (blazed a different color) that takes off to the left—stay STRAIGHT AHEAD. Eventually you will top out and pass through a couple more wildflower glades and back to the trail intersection—go STRAIGHT AHEAD to get back to the trailhead. If you have the time, be sure and visit the Bear Cave Trail just across the highway—a short excursion through very interesting rock formations.

Emergency contact: Yell County Sheriff, 479–495–2811

Ouachita Region Waterfalls

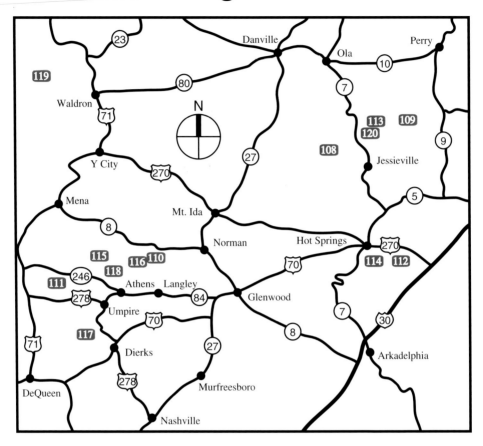

The Ouachitas are not known for their waterfalls, but there are a couple of really spectacular ones there, plus a number of others that are easy to get to and view. I'm not sure why waterfalls don't grow well in this land of rugged mountains—there is plenty of water and lots of height in the hills. I suspect it is because the rock layers that were pushed up millions of years ago now live at odd angles and don't provide the nice flat blufflines for streams to pour off to create waterfalls like the rock layers in the Ozarks do. Still, there is some great scenery to be had in our southern forest. You will see many more pine trees than in the Ozarks—that means a lot more color in the wintertime. I especially like the salt-and-pepper look of the mixed forest in the spring, when the new green growth of the hardwoods contrasts with the darker greens of the pines. If you are new to the waterfall-hunting game, I recommend that you begin with the waterfalls in the Ouachitas, then work your way up north.

Fall #	Name	Beauty Rating	Height	Hike Difficulty	Page #
108	Blocker Creek Cascade	★★★	17	Medium	216
109	Brown Creek Cascade	★★+	8	Easy	220
110	Crooked Creek Falls	★★★	16	Easy	202
111	Cossatot Falls	★★★★★	cascades	Easy	208
112	Falls Creek Falls	★★★+	12	Easy	212
113	Forked Mtn. Falls	★★★+	10	Easy	218
114	Garvan Gardens Falls	★★★+	11	Easy	214
115	Katy Falls	★★★	12	Difficult	204
116	Little Missouri Falls	★★★★	cascades	Easy	202
117	Panther Bluff Falls	★★★★	31	Easy	210
118	Shady Lake Cascade	★★★★	27	Easy	206
119	Slate Falls	★★★★+	54	Medium	200
120	Twist Cascade	★★★	12	Medium	218

Slate Falls – ★★★★+ – 54′

4.6 miles roundtrip, medium hike/bushwhack, GPS recommended
Lat/Lon–34 58.998 N, 94 16.304 W • UTM–3 **83** 941 E, 38 **71** 720 N, Cauthron Quad

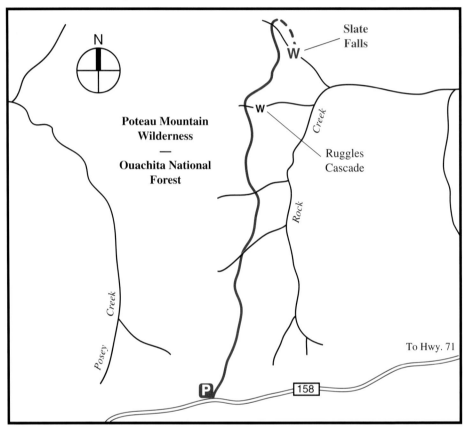

SLATE FALLS. This is far and away the tallest waterfall in the Ouachitas, and very few folks have ever seen it in modern times. An easy hike along an old logging road takes you most of the way, but the last couple hundred yards is a bushwhack down *steep* and rocky terrain. The old road is not maintained and may be blocked with numerous downed trees. Danny Ruggles grew up in these hills and said that they used to shower under this falls, and had to use a piece of slate rock to hold over their heads to keep from being pounded to death—hence the name (the cascade nearby is named after him). There is a really neat stone structure at the base of the falls that reminds me of the Indian dwellings at Mesa Verde in Colorado. The roof caved in long ago as pieces of the bluff crumbled away.

To get to the parking area from Waldron, take Hwy. 71 north—TURN LEFT onto FR#158/CR#70/Poteau Mtn. Road and zero your odometer there (this will be 2.9 miles north of the Hwy. 71 & Hwy. 28 intersection, and 4.7 miles south of the Hwy. 71 & Hwy. 23 intersection). Take the RIGHT fork after .3 mile (gravel) and continue through a residential area and then into the national forest. This road will climb *up* the southern spine of the Poteau Mountains, and you will have many terrific long views. There is a picnic table or two along the way, but keep your eye on the road because it gets a little hairy. The Poteau Mountain Wilderness will be on your right. PARK at 11.7—there is an open area on both sides of the road with a great view to the south.

Slate Falls (high water—photo taken during downpour!)

An old road takes off to the north (right side of the road) at the back of a deer camp there—you will follow this old road all the way to near the top of the waterfall. The road eases down the hill just a little, winds around a bit, levels out, and crosses several small creeks. At about 1.7 you will come to a creek, and will be in an area where the forest is mostly pine trees. (If you want a side trip leave the road here and bushwhack down the stream a couple of hundred *steep* yards to Ruggles Cascade, a neat area of tumbling water—34 58.721 N, 94 16.4148 W/ 3 **83** 766 E, 38 **71** 210 N.) Continue on the old road as it curves around to the left, and at about 2.2 you will come to another creek that should be flowing well. There will be lots of cedar trees mixed in with the pines here, and you will be in an obvious drainage. *Cross* the creek and LEAVE THE ROAD to the right and bush-whack down alongside the creek until you come to the falls. There is an easy way down to the base of the falls on that side, and you can go take a look at the old stone homesite.

Emergency contact: Sebastian County Sheriff, 479–783–1051

Little Missouri Falls – ★★★★ – cascades
.25 mile roundtrip, easy short hike, GPS not needed
Lat/Lon–34 25.297 N, 93 55.125 W • UTM–4 **15** 592 E, 38 **9** 080 N, Big Fork Quad

Crooked Creek Falls – ★★★ – 16'
Located next to the road, no hike, GPS not needed
Lat/Lon–34 25.620 N, 93 53.135 W • UTM–4 **18** 644 E, 38 **9** 651 N, Big Fork Quad

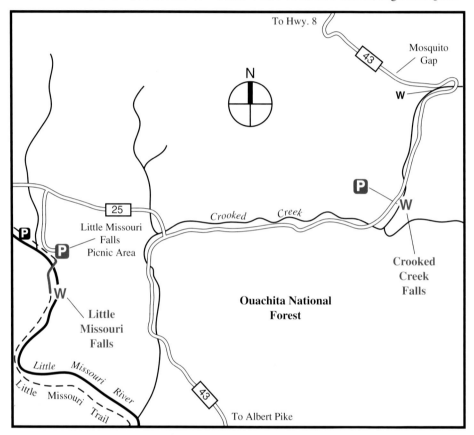

LITTLE MISSOURI FALLS/CROOKED CREEK FALLS. There are many different ways to get to this area—both falls are close to each other and require little or no hiking to view.

From Langley (west from Glenwood on Hwy. 70 and then west on Hwy. 84) take Hwy. 369 six miles to Albert Pike Recreation Area. Continue straight through the campground as the road turns to FR#73 (gravel), and follow it about three miles and TURN LEFT onto FR#43. Go 4.3 miles to the intersection with FR#25 (you will have been driving through the Crooked Creek Gorge for the past .5 mile—lots of nice cascades!). To get to Crooked Creek Falls continue STRAIGHT AHEAD 1.4 miles and PARK along the road—the falls will be just down to the right. To get to Little Missouri Falls from the intersection above, TURN LEFT onto FR#25 and go .7 mile and TURN LEFT at the big sign, which will take you down into the picnic area where you park. The paved trail takes off there and crosses the creek on a stepping-stone bridge of sorts (careful during high water!) and goes to a pair of overlooks with good views of the cascade area.

Little Missouri Falls (above), **Crooked Creek Falls** (below, during high water)

From Norman take Hwy. 8 west 12.7 miles and TURN LEFT onto FR#43. Go 3.3 miles and PARK—Crooked Creek Falls will be down on your left. Continue on another 1.4 miles and TURN RIGHT on FR#25, then TURN LEFT after .7 mile to get to Little Missouri Falls. If the water is high you will need lots of film!

Emergency contact: Montgomery County Sheriff, 870–867–3151

Katy Falls – ★★★ – 12′

9.6 mile loop, medium backpack or difficult dayhike, GPS helpful
Lat/Lon–34 23.815 N, 94 04.818 W • UTM–4 **00** 716 E, 38 **06** 487 N, Nichols Mtn. Quad

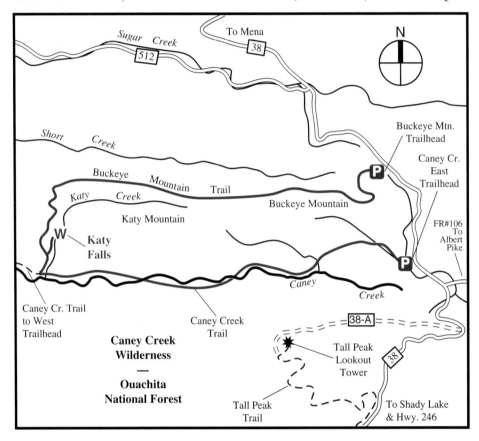

KATY FALLS. The 14,433-acre Caney Creek Wilderness area is the oldest one in Arkansas, and contains the first backpacking trail built in the state. When I taught backpacking 101 at the University of Arkansas back in the mid-1970's we used to come to Caney Creek for our weekend hikes, and Katy Falls was always one of the highlights. It is a pretty small falls, but well worth the side trip if you are hiking Caney. My favorite trip here now is to make a loop, starting with the Buckeye Mountain Trail, which has some terrific views, and coming out via the Caney Creek Trail. It's a great overnight trip, or a very long dayhike. The alternate route is shorter, but less scenic. It starts/ends at the East Caney Creek Trailhead and follows the Caney Creek Trail to the falls and back out via the same route.

To get to the Buckeye Mountain Trailhead for the big loop, take Hwy. 246 west from Athens a couple miles and TURN RIGHT onto FR#38 towards Shady Lake. Continue past Shady Lake, past the turnoff up to Tall Peak, past the turnoff to Bard Springs/Albert Pike, past the East Caney Creek Trailhead (park here for the alternate route), and continue on up to the top of the hill and PARK on the left at the Buckeye Mountain Trailhead after about eight or nine miles from Hwy. 246.

The Buckeye Mountain Trail heads out into the woods and climbs gradually up and around Buckeye Mountain. It enters a high land of rocky outcrops, giant trees, and some

Katy Falls (it looks bigger in real life!)

terrific views. The trail does a lot of up-and-downing as it follows along near the top of a long ridge, dodging those many rock outcrops, knobs, and various other geological features. You'll find a lot of wildflowers in the open areas here in the spring and early summer. And did I say great views? The hills just seem to go on forever.

At 3.4 the trail TURNS LEFT, leaves the ridgetop, and begins a rapid descent down into the Katy and Caney Creek drainages. Just before you hit bottom at 4.5, TURN LEFT on a little spur trail. This runs alongside Katy Creek a couple hundred yards to the falls. There are a number of good campsites along Caney Creek, which is just down the main trail at 4.6, but this area really gets pounded with campers and many great sites have been closed.

To continue with the loop, TURN LEFT at the bottom of the hill at 4.6 when you hit the Caney Creek Trail. That hike out to the trailhead is 3.9 miles and follows along Caney Creek upstream most of the way, crossing it a couple of times. There is one good climb along the north side of the creek, and one last climb out of the drainage, and then you drop on down to the East Caney Creek Trailhead at 8.5. TURN LEFT and follow the forest road 1.1 miles back up the hill to complete the loop.

To do the alternate route (7.8 miles total), PARK at the East Caney Creek Trailhead and hike the Caney Creek Trail 3.9 miles to the falls and back out the same way. You will cross the creek several times each way, so plan on wet feet.

Emergency contact: Polk County Sheriff, 479–394–2511

Shady Lake Cascade – ★★★★ – 27′

View from your car, GPS not needed

Lat/Lon–34 21.576 N, 94 01.686 W • UTM–4 **05** 473 E, 38 **02** 299 N, Umpire Quad

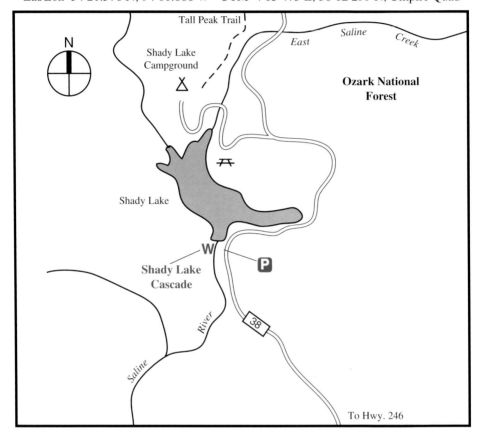

SHADY LAKE CASCADE. This really neat cascade is located just off to the side of the Shady Lake dam and spillway. There is a small pulloff that overlooks the spot, so no need to even hike in order to see it. Lots of campsites at the lake, plus a picnic area, swimming area, and a trailhead for the Tall Peak Trail.

To get to Shady Lake take Hwy. 246 west out of Athens 2.2 miles and TURN RIGHT onto FR#38. Go 2.9 miles to Shady Lake and pull off and PARK on the left at the overlook. You can see the cascade, the spillway, and the emerald creek below from there.

While you are in the area you might want to take the drive up to Tall Peak (or hike the trail up to it that begins in the campground)—just continue on FR#38 for several miles and turn left when you get to the top of the hill. There is an old historic lookout tower there. This little hilltop is absolutely *covered* with spiderworts in the spring!

Emergency contact: Polk County Sheriff, 479–394–2511

Shady Lake Cascade

Cossatot Falls – ★★★★★ – cascades

Up to 1.0 mile roundtrip, easy/medium hike, GPS not needed

Lat/Lon–34 19.168 N, 94 13.606 W • UTM–3 **87** 149 E, 37 **98** 052 N, Baker Springs Quad

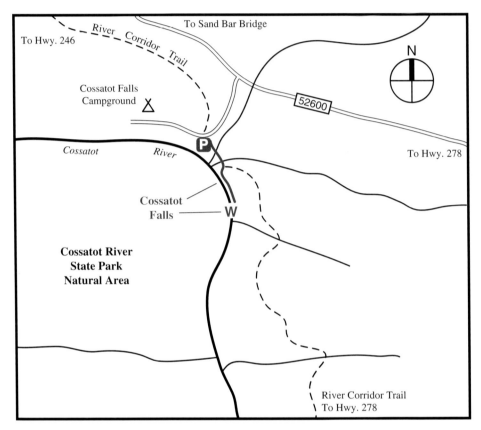

COSSATOT FALLS. Wow, this is one incredible spot that you must see! It has been long known as one of the best kayak playgrounds around, but more and more folks are discovering it for the pure scenic beauty it possesses. It is not really a waterfall, but rather a quarter-mile long series of cascades that roar and splash through many boulders that have been polished smooth by the powerful action of the Cossatot River (the name means "skull crusher," and it lives up to that name quite well). This area is terrific to visit even when the water is low—the sculptured rocks are really something to see, plus there is a great swimming hole or two downstream. The park is jointly managed by Arkansas State Parks and Arkansas Natural Heritage Commission, and contains 11 miles of the river and more than 5,000 acres. All of this is surrounded by paper company land, so you will see lots of tree farms being clearcut as you come and go, but you won't see any of this from the river itself. There will be future development at the park, including more hiking trails and a nice Visitor/Education Center. For now there is primitive camping available at several sites, including where we park to visit the falls, and a 14-mile long hiking trail.

To get to the parking area from Glenwood, take Hwy. 70 west and TURN RIGHT onto Hwy. 84 to Langley, Athens and Umpire, then TURN RIGHT onto Hwy. 278 at Umpire. Go 6.6 miles and TURN RIGHT onto paper company road #52600 (gravel—

Cossatot Falls

watch for log trucks!). Go 4.6 miles and TURN LEFT into the Cossatot Falls Recreation Area and park at the restroom. By the way, as you drive along please remember that we are all consumers of trees every single day of our lives (they make toilet paper and houses from them you know), and tree farming is one of the best ways to produce enough to keep up with our demand! You can also get to the falls area via Hwy. 246 to the north, but the road is longer and rougher—the turnoff is located between Athens and Vandervoort.

NOTE: If the water levels are high, you may need to take a different road off of the highway. Instead of turning right onto road #52600 from Hwy. 278, CONTINUE south on the highway, across a bridge over Baker Creek, to the next road, which will be #52200 (both roads are signed for Cossatot River interior access). TURN RIGHT on this road and follow it for about 3.5 miles and then TURN LEFT onto #52600, then LEFT into the campground. This route will take you around a ford of Baker Creek that might be flooded.

There isn't a good way to construct an actual trail along the river to see the falls area, but there is a path of sorts that you can follow from the parking area. How difficult/safe this route will be depends a great deal on the level of the river. There is also a hiking trail that leaves the parking area and climbs the hills above the river, and you can get some views of the falls area from the trail during leaf-off periods. This is the river-length trail in the park that goes upstream from Hwy. 246 and downstream to Hwy. 278.

To view the falls up close, take the trail from the parking area across the two monster trail bridges. At the far end of the second bridge the hiking trail goes to the left and immediately climbs up the hill. You want to stay on the level and GO STRAIGHT ahead to the banks of the river. From that point on it is a scramble to find your way. At some point downstream your route will be blocked by a wall of rock and you will have to turn back.

Emergency contact: Howard County Sheriff, 479–845–2626

Panther Bluff Falls – ★★★★ – 31′

Short hike from car, GPS not needed

Lat/Lon–34 11.744 N, 94 05.040 W • UTM–4 **00** 138 E, 37 **84** 182 N, Dierks Dam Quad

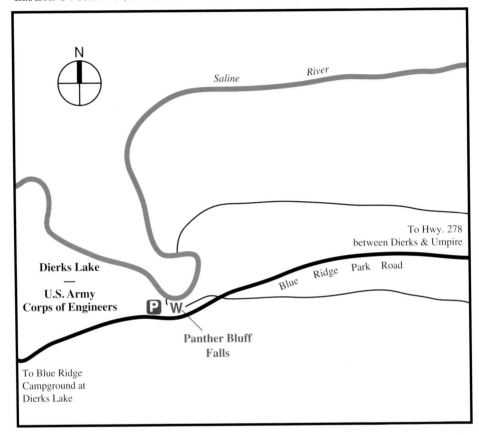

PANTHER BLUFF FALLS. I was somewhat surprised the day I pulled over to see this waterfall for the first time—it's a very nice little waterfall right there next to the road! And it is taller than most waterfalls in the Ouachitas. There is also a smaller falls just below this one, but the scramble down to see it is kind of dangerous, and you might end up in the Saline River if you slip. (I can speak from personal experience on that one—just before I took the photo at right I slipped and fell over the lower bluff!)

    From Athens take Hwy. 84 six miles to Umpire and TURN LEFT onto Hwy. 278. Go 7.0 miles and TURN RIGHT onto Blue Ridge Park Road (this will be just after you cross over the Saline River bridge). Go 2.2 miles and PARK on the right. The waterfall is located just down the hill to the right. There is a small creek there running alongside the highway that spills over Panther Bluff, which is made up of many thin layers of shale. Right down below is the Saline River (it is actually considered the upper end of Dierks Lake at this point).

    From Dierks go east on Hwy. 70 about three miles and TURN LEFT onto Hwy. 278. After four miles or so and just before you cross the Saline River Bridge, TURN LEFT onto Blue Ridge Park Road, then go 2.2 miles and PARK.

    Emergency contact: Howard County Sheriff, 479–845–2626

Panther Bluff Falls

Falls Creek Falls – ★★★+ – 12′
1.4 miles roundtrip, easy hike, GPS not needed
Lat/Lon–34 25.519 N, 92 54.682 W • UTM–5 **08** 160 E, 38 **09** 112 N, Lake Catherine Quad

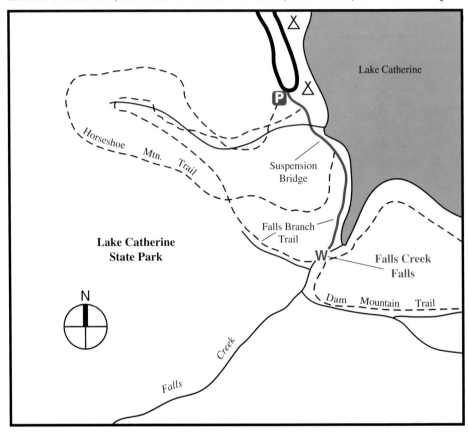

FALLS CREEK FALLS. You've probably seen this waterfall in dozens of photographs—it is one of the favorite falls used to advertise Arkansas State Parks. The hike to the falls is an easy stroll along the lake shore. If you are feeling energetic, you can hike several different loop trails that connect with this one for a total hike of 6.3 miles. But we'll just stick with the short hike to the base of the falls and back. By the way, the name of the creek is Falls "Creek" and the waterfall is Falls "Creek" Falls, but the name of the trail is Falls "Branch" Trail. Also, they tell me another name for the waterfall is Devil's Bathtub. I don't know what the fascination with the term "Devil" is in relation to waterfalls, but we have several with that reference in Arkansas (Devil's Den, Devils Canyon, Devils Fork). I suspect some of it may be that the watercourses that go along with the falls are very tough.

From Hot Springs, take Hwy. 270 east and TURN RIGHT onto Carpenter Dam Road (Hwy. 28), then LEFT on Hwy. 290, then LEFT again on Hwy. 171 and follow it all the way into the park. From Little Rock, take I–30 south to exit 97 near Malvern, then go north on Hwy. 171 until you reach the park. The trailhead is located at the back of the park, just past the amphitheater. This is a fully-equipped campground with plenty of sites here, but you may find the constant drone of the powerhouse across the lake a bit annoying.

Falls Creek Falls

There are several trails that take off from the trailhead, but the one you want is the Falls Creek Trail that goes down near the lake shore. It heads out through some nice big trees, crosses a road near the camping area, and goes over a foot bridge—we are following the white blazes. (There are actually three different trails that share the first part of this route, so you will see different colored blazes on the trees). The trail begins to follow the lake shore, then at .4 crosses a nice suspension bridge. Just beyond it we come to an intersection— continue STRAIGHT AHEAD and along the lake.

Soon the trail curves around to the right and heads up into a small cove, and to the waterfall at .7. The trails continue from this point, one crossing the creek above the falls and looping around a hill and back to the same point, another trail follows a little stream (or "branch") uphill and then eventually back to the trailhead. You can take your pick of them all and spend a good part of your day hiking here, or simply head back the way you came and go find another waterfall!

Emergency: Hot Spring County Sheriff, 501–332–3671; Park office, 501–844–4176.

Garvan Gardens Falls – ★★★+ – 11′

300 yards roundtrip (fee required), easy hike, GPS not needed
Lat/Lon–34 26.011 N, 93 2.803 W • UTM–4 **95** 724 E, 38 **10** 19 N, Hot Springs S. Quad

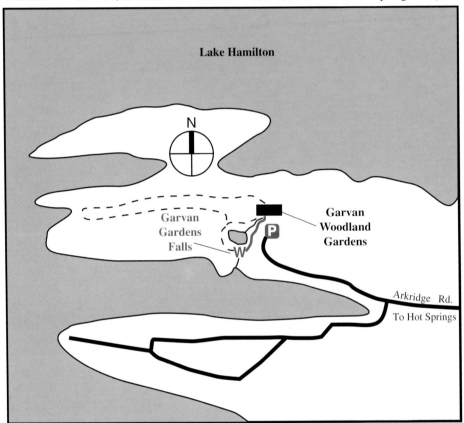

GARVAN GARDENS FALLS. I don't normally send folks to man-made waterfalls or places where an entrance fee is charged, but while Garvan Woodland Gardens has both, it is such a wonderful place that I just had to include it in this guidebook. The gardens are owned by the University of Arkansas, and they have a long and colorful history. Besides the main waterfall and interesting features fashioned with water and stone (including a really neat arched bridge made of stone), there are literally thousands of blooming plants all over the place, and many trails that wind through the 210-acre property. It is open most days of the year, except for some of the major holidays—call 800–366–4664 or visit them online at www.garvangardens.org for more information.

To get to the gardens from Hot Springs take the Carpenter Dam Exit (Hwy. 28) off Hwy. 270 bypass and head south for five miles, then TURN RIGHT on Arkridge Road until you come to the garden entrance. The waterfall is one of the first things you will see if you hike the trail down the hill in a clockwise direction. They built a unique little step-across bridge at the bottom of this falls that is actually two rocks facing each other. I recommend that you plan to spend at least a couple of hours wandering around and enjoying this place. Take a special companion along and hold hands a lot!

Emergency contact: Garland County Sheriff, 501–622–3690

Garvan Woodland Gardens Falls

Blocker Creek Cascade – ★★★ – 17′

1.0 mile roundtrip, easy hike plus medium bushwhack, GPS helpful
Lat/Lon–34 43.933 N, 93 12.710 W • UTM–4 **80** 623 E, 38 **43** 161 N, Hamilton Quad

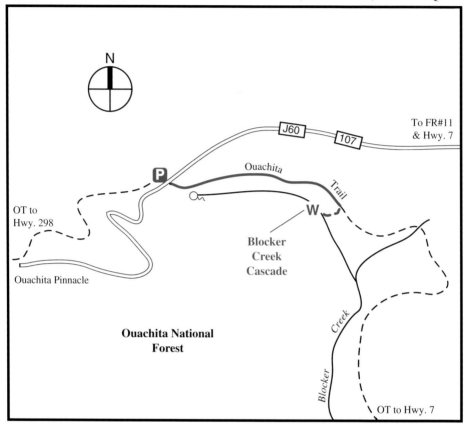

BLOCKER CREEK CASCADE. There aren't many waterfalls high in the Ouachitas, but this is a nice treat tucked away in the extreme headwaters of Blocker Creek. And once you make the drive up to Blue Ouachita Mountain to get to it, you can drive just a little bit farther and take in the view from Ouachita Pinnacle.

To get to the parking area from Jessieville, take Hwy. 7 north about seven miles, past the Iron Springs Recreation Area, and about .5 mile past the big parking lot to the Ouachita Trail, then TURN LEFT onto FR#11 (gravel). [This turnoff is located just across the highway from the Winona Forest Drive (FR#132) that heads back to the east and is a beautiful drive along the southern boundary of the Flatside Wilderness area and connects to Hwy. 9.] From the highway go about 6.5 miles and TURN LEFT onto FR#J60 (gravel). Follow this road 3.6 miles up the hill (it becomes FR#107) and PARK where the Ouachita Trail crosses the road. NOTE: parts of FR#107 shown on some maps are now closed.

Get on the Ouachita Trail (which is an old roadbed at this point) and head south (to the left). You will be dropping gradually down the hillside and should see and hear a small stream down the hill on your right—the waterfall is located on that stream. If you don't have a GPS, your best bet is to simply leave the trail after a couple hundred yards, get down to the stream, and follow it until you come to the waterfall—only about .25 mile

Blocker Creek Cascade
(This photo was taken in 2002 and shows the extreme damage from recent ice storms—the view should be better in the future!)

from where you parked. If you have a GPS, stay on the trail until you come above the falls, then bushwhack down to it. The hillside is very steep!

Emergency contact: Garland County Sheriff, 501–622–3690

Forked Mountain Falls – ★★★+ – 10′

1.6 miles roundtrip, easy hike, GPS helpful

Lat/Lon–34 51.298 N, 93 01.845 W • UTM–4 **97** 204 E, 38 **56** 753 N, Nimrod SE Quad

Twist Cascade – ★★★ – 12′

Add 1.6 miles to above distance, easy bushwhack, GPS helpful

Lat/Lon–34 50.961 N, 93 02.140 W • UTM–4 **96** 755 E, 38 **56** 130 N, Nimrod SE Quad

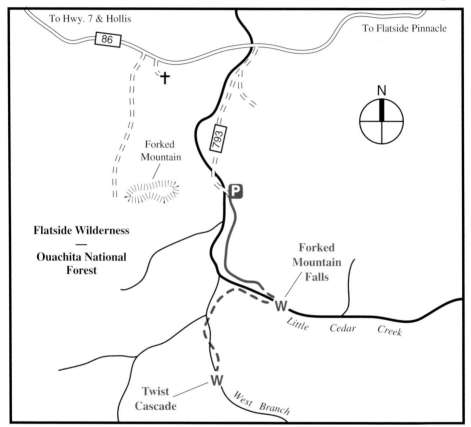

FORKED MOUNTAIN FALLS/TWIST CASCADE. Here are a couple of nice little falls in the shadow of Forked Mountain, which is my favorite mountain in Arkansas.

To get to the parking area, take FR#86 (gravel) east from Hwy. 7 (the turn is located just south of Hollis, and north of Jessieville). Go 4.7 miles and TURN RIGHT onto FR#793. Go .9 mile (cross the creek twice) and PARK at a locked gate at the wilderness boundary.

Hike along the closed road, up and over a couple of humps, then veer off to the RIGHT on an old road trace at about .7—this old trace will take you over to Forked Mountain Falls. There is a nice pool of water there—hum, perhaps a quick dip?

To get to the cascade, either cross the stream or go downstream and cross on an old road trace that has become really grown up. Follow this trace across level ground until it comes to a small creek—cross there and stay on the old trace as it curves back to the left, then cross the stream again. The trace swings back to the right and uphill a little and comes alongside Twist Cascade which you will be able to see and hear below to the right.

Emergency contact: Saline County Sheriff, 501–303–5603

Forked Mountain Falls
(above, with my
daughter Amber)

Twist Cascade (right)

Brown Creek Cascade – ★★+ – 8'

.5 mile roundtrip, easy hike, GPS not needed

Lat/Lon–34 51.921 N, 92 53.353 W • UTM–5 **10** 141 E, 38 **57** 909 N, Paron SW Quad

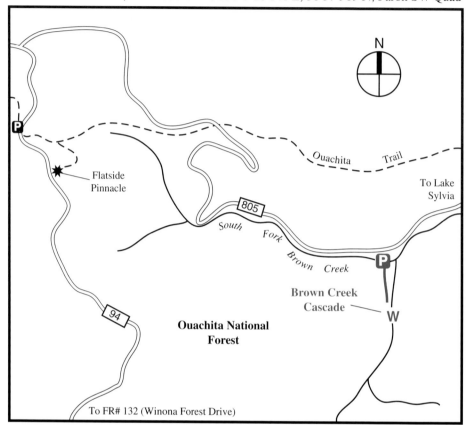

BROWN CREEK CASCADE. There are hundreds of little cascades like this one in the Ozarks, but not many of them in the Ouachitas. I decided to include this one in the guide because it is so easy to get to, and is close to Little Rock. It will be a big disappointment to most waterfall chasers, but it is actually a nice little cascade and a great destination for first-time waterfall hunters. It is especially great for kids as the hike to it is easy, and the cascade is "just their size." It's also a nice stop on the way to Flatside Pinnacle to view the sunset. Look for lots of wildflowers along the way in April and May.

To get to the parking spot TURN EAST onto Hwy. 324 (paved) from Hwy. 9 towards Lake Sylvia (this turn is just north of Williams Junction of Hwys 9 & 10, and south of Perryville). Go 1.7 miles and TURN RIGHT onto FR#805/Brown Creek Road (gravel). Go 5.3 miles and PARK in a little camp area on the left.

There is an old road trace (closed) that takes off from this camp area and immediately crosses Brown Creek. Stay on this road trace just a couple of hundred yards and you will come to the little cascade on the left.

If you want a quick hike up to one of the best sunset views in Arkansas, continue along FR#805 another 2.8 miles then TURN LEFT on FR#94 and take it on up to a big parking area at the base of Flatside Pinnacle. Park there and take the Ouachita Trail to the

Brown Creek Cascade

east, up the hill a quarter mile, to an intersection with a spur trail that swings on up to the right and ends at the top edge of Flatside Pinnacle. There isn't too much room up there and the footing can be tricky, but the view to the west is wonderful! (See page 81 in my *Arkansas Wilderness* picture book for a photo of the view.)

Emergency contact: Perry County Sheriff, 501–889–2333

Books by Tim Ernst

❏ *ARKANSAS HIKING TRAILS* $ 18.95
Maps and descriptions of 78 major trails in the state.
6" x 9", 192 pages

❏ *OZARK HIGHLANDS TRAIL GUIDE* $ 18.95
The definitive guide to this fabulous 165–mile trail.
Thirteen maps, nine elevation profiles, 5.5" x 8.5", 136 pages

❏ *BUFFALO RIVER HIKING TRAILS* $ 18.95
Maps and descriptions of over 30 trails in the river area.
5.5" x 8.5", 136 pages

❏ *ARKANSAS DAYHIKES FOR KIDS* $ 18.95
Maps and descriptions of the best dayhikes in the state for kids.

❏ *OUACHITA TRAIL GUIDE* $ 18.95
The complete guide to the longest trail in the region.
Ten maps and elevation profiles, 5.5" x 8.5", 136 pages

❏ *SWIMMING HOLE GUIDE TO THE OZARKS* (Glenn Wheeler) $ 18.95
Directions and maps to the best old time holes in Arkansas and Missouri!

❏ *THE SEARCH FOR HALEY* $ 19.95
An Insider's Account of the Largest Search Mission in Arkansas History.
5.5" x 8.5", 240 pages

❏ *ARKANSAS WATERFALL GUIDE* $ 19.95
❏ *ARKANSAS WILDERNESS* picture book $ 29.95
Contains 100 colorful images from all over the state.
9.5" x 10.5", 132 pages, soft cover, autographed

❏ *ARKANSAS SPRING* picture book $ 29.95
105 color images of dogwoods, waterfalls and wildflowers.
10.5" x 11.5", 128 pages, hardcover, gift boxed, autographed

❏ *BUFFALO RIVER WILDERNESS* picture book $ 29.95
63 photos by Ernst, 58 watercolors by William McNamara.
10.5" x 11.5", 128 pages, hardcover, gift boxed, autographed

❏ *WILDERNESS REFLECTIONS* picture book $ 29.95
121 color photographs from the best scenic areas in the land.
10.5" x 11.5", 156 pages, hardcover, gift boxed, autographed

❏ *ARKANSAS WILDERNESS* wall calendar (yearly) $ 14.95
12 stunning color photographs throughout the seasons, 12" x 12"

**Color enlargements of all the photos in this book are available
in a variety of sizes, with or without the people.**

About The Author

When I was a kid growing up at the edge of Fayetteville, I used to run out into the rain and spend hours building little mud and rock dams on the tiny streams around our house, which created miniature waterfalls. Since those early days of bliss I always get a twinkle in my eye when it rains, and seek out real waterfalls whenever I can.

Along the way I started building hiking trails and taking pictures, lots of pictures (I've photographed thousands of waterfalls all across the United States in my 30-year career as a wilderness photographer). I enjoy telling others about the many special places that we have here in Arkansas, and showing them how to get there through my many guidebooks. I firmly believe that we all have the right to view and experience the treasures of our natural world that belong to all of us.

So that is what I do in life—take pictures, write guidebooks, build hiking trails, and generally spend as much time outdoors as I can. And I try to keep up with the two ladies in my life—my wife and partner, Pam, and our daughter, Amber (that's her waterfall below). We live at the edge of the wilderness in a log cabin called Cloudland, and there are many great waterfalls nearby to explore. You can read about some of those adventures in the online *Cloudland Journal* at www.Cloudland.net. I just turned 48, and suspect I've got a few hundred more waterfalls yet to find and photograph...

Amber Falls
(text and map are on page 32)

Legend For All Maps (distance scale varies)

————	Main Route—Trail		**P**	Trailhead Parking
– – – –	Main Route—Bushwhack		**P**	Other parking
– – – –	Other Trails or Routes		**W**	Main Waterfall
- - - - - -	Alternate Bushwhack Route		**W**	Other Waterfall

≈ Creek, Streams, Rivers

⌒ ⋎ Spring, Cave

✳ Point of Interest

△ �🪑 Campground, Picnic Area

———— Paved Highway

✝ Cemetery

═══════ Gravel Forest Road

(71) Paved Highway

= = = = = Jeep Road

(23) (341) State/County Road-Paved/Gravel

● ■ COMMUNITY/City, Building

[1003] Gravel Forest Road

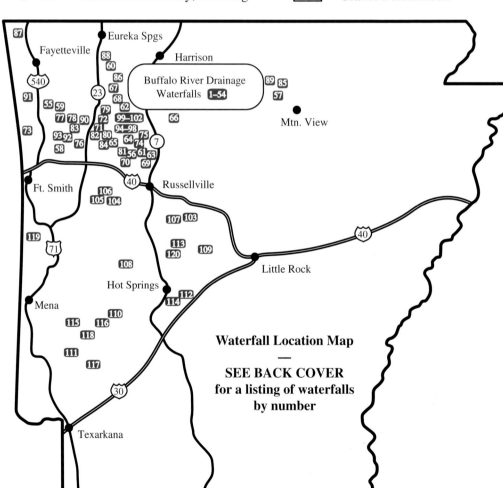

87
Eureka Spgs
Fayetteville
88
60
86 Harrison
540 67 Buffalo River Drainage 89 85
91 23 68 Waterfalls 1-54 57
55 59 62
77 78 90 79 72 99-102 66
73 83 71 94-98 Mtn. View
93 92 82 80 64 75
58 84 65 74
81 56 61 7
70 69 63

Ft. Smith 40 Russellville
106
105 104

107 103

119
71 113 40
120 109
108 Little Rock

Hot Springs 112
Mena 114
110
115 116
118
111
117

Waterfall Location Map
—
SEE BACK COVER
for a listing of waterfalls
by number

30

Texarkana